CAMBRIDGE LIB

Books of endu

MW00805827

Music

The systematic academic study of music gave rise to works of description, analysis and criticism, by composers and performers, philosophers and anthropologists, historians and teachers, and by a new kind of scholar - the musicologist. This series makes available a range of significant works encompassing all aspects of the developing discipline.

The Third or Transition Period of Musical History

The music teacher and composer John Pyke Hullah (1812–84) is best remembered for his 'singing school for schoolmasters'. Through his dedicated efforts music was embedded into the school curriculum, and his inspiration influenced the rapid growth of amateur choral societies in Britain. Professor of vocal music at King's College, London, from 1844 to 1874, Hullah was elected to the committee of management of the Royal Academy of Music in 1869 and in 1872 became the first government inspector of music in teacher training colleges. The work reissued here is the second edition, published in 1876, of lectures given at the Royal Institution in 1865 on the topic of Italian, French, German and English music from the Renaissance to Handel. It expands on part of his overarching 1861 course of lectures, *The History of Modern Music*, which is also reissued in this series.

Cambridge University Press has long been a pioneer in the reissuing of out-of-print titles from its own backlist, producing digital reprints of books that are still sought after by scholars and students but could not be reprinted economically using traditional technology. The Cambridge Library Collection extends this activity to a wider range of books which are still of importance to researchers and professionals, either for the source material they contain, or as landmarks in the history of their academic discipline.

Drawing from the world-renowned collections in the Cambridge University Library and other partner libraries, and guided by the advice of experts in each subject area, Cambridge University Press is using state-of-the-art scanning machines in its own Printing House to capture the content of each book selected for inclusion. The files are processed to give a consistently clear, crisp image, and the books finished to the high quality standard for which the Press is recognised around the world. The latest print-on-demand technology ensures that the books will remain available indefinitely, and that orders for single or multiple copies can quickly be supplied.

The Cambridge Library Collection brings back to life books of enduring scholarly value (including out-of-copyright works originally issued by other publishers) across a wide range of disciplines in the humanities and social sciences and in science and technology.

The Third or
Transition Period
of Musical History

A Course of Lectures Delivered at
the Royal Institution of Great Britain

JOHN HULLAH

CAMBRIDGE
UNIVERSITY PRESS

University Printing House, Cambridge, CB2 8BS, United Kingdom

Published in the United States of America by Cambridge University Press, New York

Cambridge University Press is part of the University of Cambridge.

It furthers the University's mission by disseminating knowledge in the pursuit of
education, learning and research at the highest international levels of excellence.

www.cambridge.org
Information on this title: www.cambridge.org/9781108063982

© in this compilation Cambridge University Press 2013

This edition first published 1876
This digitally printed version 2013

ISBN 978-1-108-06398-2 Paperback

This book reproduces the text of the original edition. The content and language reflect
the beliefs, practices and terminology of their time, and have not been updated.

Cambridge University Press wishes to make clear that the book, unless originally published
by Cambridge, is not being republished by, in association or collaboration with, or
with the endorsement or approval of, the original publisher or its successors in title.

THE THIRD

TRANSITION PERIOD OF MUSICAL HISTORY.

THE

THIRD OR TRANSITION PERIOD

OF

MUSICAL HISTORY.

𝔄 Course of Lectures

DELIVERED AT THE

ROYAL INSTITUTION OF GREAT BRITAIN.

BY

J O H N   H U L L A H,

HONORARY FELLOW OF KING'S COLLEGE;
PROFESSOR OF VOCAL MUSIC IN QUEEN'S COLLEGE AND IN BEDFORD COLLEGE, LONDON;
AND ORGANIST OF CHARTERHOUSE.

SECOND EDITION.

LONDON:

LONGMANS, GREEN, AND CO.

1876.

LONDON :
SAVILL, EDWARDS AND CO., PRINTERS, CHANDOS STREET,
COVENT GARDEN.

TO

THE RIGHT HONOURABLE

WILLIAM EWART GLADSTONE, M.P.

CHANCELLOR OF THE EXCHEQUER

THIS VOLUME IS INSCRIBED

WITH THE RESPECT AND GRATITUDE OF

THE AUTHOR.

May, 1865.

PREFACE

THE FIRST EDITION.

———

THIS Course of Lectures stands in the same relation to that which I delivered at the Royal Institution in 1861, as a topographical map to a geographical. I have here treated a portion of a subject which there I had only been enabled to treat generally, with some attention to detail, and with comparative completeness. I say " comparative ;" because no one can be more fully alive to his " sins of omission" in the present instance than I am. The horizon of the historical student is for ever enlarging ; and every fresh fact, work, or person that comes upon it, introduces him to others of whose importance—sometimes of whose existence—he had no previous conception.

In one respect at least this Course will be more valuable, and of greater interest, than my former one,—in being accompanied by so many, and such beautiful, musical illustrations. These, for the most part, consist of pieces never before printed in this country, some of which indeed had existed heretofore only in manuscript. The majority will certainly be new to all but the most enterprising of musical antiquaries.

It is possible that the praises I have bestowed on many of

these pieces will seem excessive, to those who make their first acquaintance with them through the eye. Addressed as they were, on the delivery of my lectures, to the ear, the very reverse was assuredly the case. And, on this account, I have a large debt of gratitude to acknowledge.

For their assistance in the vocal illustrations, I have to thank Miss Banks, Miss Martin, Miss Palmer, Mr. Wilbye Cooper, and Mr. Lewis Thomas; for the various parts they took in the concerted instrumental pieces, my acknowledgments are likewise due to Messrs. Alfred Nicholson, Watson, Zerbini, Webb, S. Webb, Severn, and Edward Howell; as also to Mr. Henry Deacon and Mr. Lindsay Sloper, for their presentations of the several pianoforte—or rather, harpsichord—solos. Nor ought I to leave unmentioned many most kind offers of assistance I received—among them one from Madame Sainton-Dolby—of which limited time and other circumstances prevented my availing myself.

Those who were present when the agency of these able and willing artists caused the long " slumbering strains," only recorded in the following pages, to " wake into voice," were not slow in expressing their admiration of the result of it. This admiration will of necessity have been increased by the consideration that the majority of the pieces performed were of a kind, and in a style, to which contemporary performers are somewhat unaccustomed. English musicians are, however, distinguished for their versatility; none are called upon, even in their ordinary practice, to deal with so great a variety of music. If the artists of other countries often excel in this or that speciality, those of our own are, as a rule, wider in their range,—quicker, because more frequent readers of new works, and superior in general musical accomplishment.

I have indicated, as the necessity or occasion for doing so presented itself, the sources of much of the information contained in the following pages, and named the works from which most of the musical excerpts have been made. For the adaptation (mostly from the German) of English words I am generally responsible; the exceptions being those of Handel's " Passion," the English text of which—a labour of love undertaken for the German Handel Society—is by Mr. Russell Martineau, and the " Passions-Musik" of Bach, Miss H. F. H. Johnston's translation of which is likely to prove inseparable from the notes with which it is associated in Professor Sterndale Bennett's admirable edition. To the author of the former, and the proprietor of the latter, work, Mr. Lamborn Cock, I am indebted for permission to make free use of both.

I have only to express a hope that the publication of this volume may do something to promote catholicity of taste among my musical contemporaries, artist or amateur; inducing them to avail themselves more freely of the inheritance their predecessors have bequeathed to them—an inheritance with the richness and variety of which the majority of them would appear to be but imperfectly acquainted.

J. H.

May, 1865.

PREFACE

THE SECOND EDITION.

———

I AVAIL myself of the opportunity afforded by the publication of this new edition to correct or supplement a passage which still stands (in p. 73) as it did in the first, in reference to one of the most interesting composers of the Transition Period, Pergolesi. Evidence which there is no reason to distrust has recently been found, to the effect that Pergolesi was born in 1710, and that he died in 1736, at the very early age, therefore, not of thirty-two, but of twenty-six.

J. H.

March, 1876.

CONTENTS.

LECTURE I.

PAGE

ITALY 1

LECTURE II.

ITALY (*continued*) 39

LECTURE III.

FRANCE 79

LECTURE IV.

GERMANY 125

LECTURE V.

ENGLAND 179

LECTURE VI.

ENGLAND (*continued*) 239

ILLUSTRATIONS.

		PAGE
HYMN—Ave Maria	*Arcadelt* . . .	9
ARIA PARLANTE—Lasciate mi morir	*Monteverde* . .	12
TRIO—Turbabuntur Impii	*Carissimi* . .	15
SONG—Vaghe Stelle	*Cavalli* . . .	26
DUET—Cara e dolce Libertà	*Cesti*	31
QUARTET—(Instrumental)	*Allegri* . . .	36
SOLO—Signor, dell' empia Gente	*Marcello* . . .	47
DUET—Quando tramonta il Sole	*Clari*	52
SONG—Lasciami piangere	*A. Scarlatti.* . .	61
QUARTET—Regina Angelorum	*Durante* . . .	66
SOLO—Vidit suum Dulcem Natum	*Pergolesi* . . .	75
QUARTET—Peuples, racontez	*Dumont* . . .	85
SCENE—J'ai perdu la Beauté	*Lully*	95
SONG—Roland, courez aux Armes	,, ...	103
SOLO—(Pianoforte) La Voluptueuse	*Couperin* . . .	106
QUARTET—Tendre Amour	*Rameau* . . .	111
SONG—Je l'ai planté	*Rousseau* . . .	121
SONG—Que le Jour me dure	,, . . .	123
CANTATA—The Finding of the Saviour . . .	*Schütz* . . .	132
SOLO—(Pianoforte)	*G. Muffat* . .	143
SOLO—O Abba, Father !	*Keiser.* . . .	153
RECITATIVE ⎰ Although mine Eyes . . . & AIR ⎱ Jesus, Saviour	⎰ *J. S. Bach* ⎱ . . 161 . . 163	
FANTAISIE—(Pianoforte)	*C. P. E. Bach* . 169	

			PAGE
SONG—While I listen to thy Voice	*H. Lawes*	.	187
SONG—Go, Young Man	,,	.	189
TRIO—(Instrumental)	*Jenkins*	.	194
ANTHEM—Hear, O Heavens !	*Humphreys*	.	204
SCENE—You Twice Ten Hundred Deities	*Purcell*	.	222
SONG—I attempt from Love's Sickness	,,	.	229
SONG—Full Fathom Five	,,	.	232
SONG—Come unto these Yellow Sands	,,	.	236
SELECTION from the Passion	*Handel*	.	246
SONG—Lascia ch'io pianga	,,	.	263
SONG—Il Tricerbero umiliato	,,	.	265
MARCH, from Rinaldo	,,	.	269
AIR & MINUET } From the Water Music	,,	.	271
DUET—Dagl' Amori flagellata	,,	.	278
COURANTE—(Pianoforte)	,,	.	290
SONG—Rendi il Sereno	,,	.	295
SCENE, from Semele	,,	.	297

LECTURE I.

ITALY.

DIVISION OF MUSICAL HISTORY INTO PERIODS—THEIR CHARACTERISTICS—THE PERFECT CADENCE—MUSICAL COMPOSITION IN THE MIDDLE AGES—EXPRESSION—ANTICIPATIONS OF MODERN TONALITY—ARCADELT—HYMN, "AVE MARIA"—THE RENAISSANCE—MUSICAL DECLAMATION OF THE GREEKS—THE FLORENTINE ACADEMY—MONTEVERDE—ARIA PARLANTE, "LASCIATE MI MORIR"—CARISSIMI—THE ORATORIO—TRIO, "TURBABUNTUR IMPII"—OPERA—CAVALLI—SONG, "VAGHE STELLE"—CESTI—DUETTO, "CARA E DOLCE LIBERTÀ"—INSTRUMENTAL ACCOMPANIMENT—THE VIOLIN—BASSANI AND CORELLI—ALLEGRI—HIS QUARTET FOR STRINGED INSTRUMENTS.

LECTURE I.

ITALY.

In a former Course of Lectures, delivered in this place, I gave a rapid and of necessity very incomplete account of the History of Modern Music from its earliest appreciable beginnings to the present time. I then divided modern musical history into four "Periods." To the beginning of the first of these I did not pretend to assign a date, but I considered it to have ended about the year 1400. My second period included the fifteenth and sixteenth centuries; my third the century and a half from about the year 1601 to the year 1750; and my fourth extended from about 1751 to the present time. As you will easily believe, I have had frequent occasion to review this division; I have found no reason for disturbing it. Actually, no doubt the periods of modern musical history are but two; for the word period, sometimes applied to epochs in which mere changes of style—superficial and obvious variations of form—in an art have been made, should, I think, be limited exclusively to successions, whether of centuries or of years, during which certain ascertained principles prevailed in the theory of that art and certain strongly marked peculiarities—expressions and results of this theory—showed themselves in the practice of it. In my first course I explained at some length what the principles and peculiarities which severally characterized the musical theory and practice of the second and of the fourth periods were. I cannot of course do this again now; and I must content myself with following the well known example of a late eminent physician, by advising those who want further information on this subject to "read my book." Let it suffice for the present that the great difference, obvious surely to the least cultivated ear, between the music of the fifteenth and sixteenth centuries and that of our own time—between the music of the Old Masters and that of our immediate predecessors and contemporaries—results from the former having had views of the nature of a "scale" or key which were very different from ours. From this cause it is that a number of effects, which to them were possibly pleasing, certainly tolerable, are, to those whose tastes have been formed exclusively on contemporary music, unpleasing, if not intolerable; and that, *vice versâ*, combinations which the old theorists one and all forbade, and which only the most audacious of their immediate successors hesitatingly and tentatively ventured upon, are now matters of every-day experience, and have even become essential—nay, indispensable —means of musical expression.

It is, I know, hard to believe, for instance, that the "perfect cadence" or discord of the dominant seventh and its resolution, with which everybody is now so familiar, which concludes ninety-nine pieces of modern music out of every hundred, and which presents itself so frequently—often too frequently—in every composition, long or short, grave or gay, which comes under a modern hearer's notice;—it is hard to believe, I say,

 that this effect was once not only unfamiliar, strange, and startling, but that there was a time when all the theorists in Europe combined their voices into one savage howl of indignation against the musician who first had the courage —not to like, but—*to say* he liked it. For, that his confession rather than his taste was Monteverde's great offence is very certain. For centuries before his time the theoretical and practical musicians, the scholars and the men of impulse, the learned and the unlearned, the talkers or writers and the doers (call them what you will), had been

moving, however slowly, in the same direction, but with a wall of Chinese height and breadth between them; as little influenced by, as ignorant of, one another's doings as though their aims had nothing in common; without a conception that these were really identical, and that they could never be attained without mutual sympathy and help. Not to go further into this matter, for which we have no time, it is enough to say that the modes of operation of the musical schoolmen of the Middle Ages resembled rather mathematical demonstration than anything we should now call composition; the popular musicians —the minstrels, the jongleurs and others—on the other hand, simply giving themselves up to the expression of their own impulses, alike ignorant and heedless of the dogmas of the learned. That in the passionless process of what he would have called composition, the mediæval scholar in music should strive to express anything in his own soul, any condition of his own being, can never have so much as occurred to him as possible or to be desired; that the operations of the minstrel could ever be subject to law can never so much as have occurred to *him*. It is a question whether before the time of Josquin Despres, who flourished about the end of the fifteenth century, any so-called musician had attained to anything beyond the vaguest conception of the *effect* of what he was putting upon paper. It is recorded of that great composer—and the record implies that the practice was a new one—that he was in the habit of gathering about him his pupils and friends skilled in singing, and of putting before them various combinations and successions of musical notes, in order that he might himself hear and judge *how they sounded.* No man could have known better whether or not they were what his predecessors and contemporaries were pleased to call according to rule; but the truth was dawning on Josquin that music would some day come to be tested by the ear as well as by the eye, by its operation on the affections as well as on the understanding.

To know exactly how that which he puts upon paper will sound—what will be its effect on his own ear as well as on that of others—to hear (so to speak) with his eyes—is the greatest difficulty with which a musical student has, and always will have, to deal;—indeed it is the power of all others the possession of which constitutes what in modern times is called a "musician." Long and special training, some would say rare and special gifts, are needed to enable the artist in combined sounds—polyphonic music—to be sure of the effect of that which he writes, or, what comes to the same thing, to be sure that he is representing that which he has conceived. Without this training he may no doubt put notes into juxta-position and make combinations follow one another, in a way which may be tolerable to a cultivated ear; nay, he may, by adhering to accepted rules, make music—good, bad, or indifferent, as the case may be; but he can never be sure that it is *his* music or the music he means it to be; nor can he even test the correctness or incorrectness of its execution by others. This was, I conceive, more often than not the condition of what was called a musician in the Middle Ages.

But the *popular* mediæval musician knew nothing of these difficulties. His aim was restricted to the production of melody, accompanied, if at all, by a few simple combinations and suc-cessions the effect of which admitted of easy proof. As to the melody itself, its effect would be ascertained in the very act of making it: for the mere melodist may be at once composer, performer, and auditor. As the painter sees the result of every touch on his canvas, and the sculptor of every chip on his marble, so the melodist can, if he pleases, hear the effect of every note as he joins it on to the notes which have gone before.

To express in the fewest words what I conceive to have been the state of music down to about the end of the fifteenth century, I should say that in the scholastic music there was no Art, and in the popular music no Science; whence it is that the former has ceased to please and the latter has for the most part perished utterly. Everything musical that can now give pleasure, everything that can hope to live through the day of its creation, must result from sentiment the expression of which is subject to law :—in a word, Music is both an art and a science.

The music of the sixteenth century, especially of the second half of it, presents numerous instances and affords numerous proofs of a craving, on the parts of the men of science, for more art; as indeed do some of the very few works of the men of art which have been preserved to us, of a craving for more science. The somewhat supercilious charge of want of expression, so often brought against the Old Masters, can no doubt frequently, though not universally, be proven. There is no want of that general accordance between the style of their music and the sentiment of the words to which it is set which is the first condition of musical expression. But this accordance is never more than general. That anything like that close following in music of the various changes of feeling expressed in poetry to which we moderns are habituated ever suggested itself to a composer of the second period is sufficiently disproved in one of the greatest works of the greatest of them. Palestrina has set these words, " Incipit Lamentatio Jeremiæ Prophetæ, Lectio I." (" Here beginneth the first Chapter of the Lamentations of the Prophet Jeremiah"), to music as noble and as affecting as any suggested to him by the most touching passages which follow in the " Lamentations" themselves. As a solitary instance this might not be worth much. Indeed it might admit of explanation if not justification. But all concurrent testimony, direct or indirect, is in favour of the truth of my assertion; and, more than this, the musical incidents which begin the seventeenth century prove beyond a doubt that the development of the music of the second period had reached its limits, and that advancement was only possible with a scale-system, or " tonality," based in nature, and therefore new.

It is certain that this, which the composers of the third period proved, was more than suspected by some of the most inventive of the second. A very pleasing exemplification of it, among many that might be adduced, is presented in a short composition by Arcadelt, one of the most illustrious of that body of Gallo-Belgian musicians who, in the first half of the sixteenth century, laid the foundations of what after-wards became the Roman School—the musicians, in fact, who were the teachers of Palestrina and his contemporaries. This composition is the more remarkable for its precocity, as being—not a piece of secular music, nor even of " measured" Church music, but—a piece of harmonized " plain-song,"—*i.e.*, melody in which " time" is supplemented by " rhythm," and the relative duration and emphasis of notes are subjected alto-gether to the quantity and accent of the syllables to which they are set.*

It is not without an effort that a modern musician is enabled to realize this timeless music, the traditional mode of performing which, possibly recoverable, has been for some time partially if not wholly lost. It is not by accident that we moderns invariably speak of music as consisting of time and tune— never, of tune and time. The measured, though monotonous, beats of a drum appeal far more intelligibly to our musical sense than the most varied succession of unproportionate sounds. Nevertheless, whatever its shortcomings, plain-song is a variety of music in the utter neglect of which modern practice would seem to have lost a good deal,—if only because it is a variety.

---

* No existing notation can express more than approximately the rela-tive duration of the sounds in Plain-Song,—the so-called " Gregorian" notation no more than our own. In the accompanying copy the semi-breves, minims, crotchets, and quavers must not be estimated according to their usual relative value; they must be regarded only as indicating notes to be performed *somewhat* quicker or slower than one another. The words are the only safe guide in the performance of this kind of music.

HYMN.—AVE MARIA.

ARCADELT.

I have not presented this Hymn of Arcadelt as an average specimen of the music of his epoch, but as an exceptional one. The vocal music of the second period was generally characterized by breadth, coherence, and high finish; but for the most part it seems to us vague, from the continual overlapping of one phrase by another, and inconsequent, from its unsatisfactory "tonality;" a piece, as a modern musician would say, often or generally ending in a different scale or key from that in which it began, or, what is worse, ending with a half-close, or "imperfect cadence,"—leaving the hearer in expectation that the composer is going to say something more, when, as it proves, he has said all he has to say, and has, wisely of course, come to end. Music like this, though still, on account of its beautiful texture, always performed with pleasure, and generally listened to with respect—for though it may be sometimes dull it is never trite —was far from realizing the ideal of the new race of scholars and savants engendered by that astonishing, and for the time irresistible force—the Renaissance.

I have on a former occasion given an outline of the action of the Renaissance of Music—the last of the arts affected by it: how certain Florentine gentlemen and scholars, united and stimulated by their love of poetry and music, set to work to re-unite these too long dissevered powers; how similar and possibly unconnected essays were made at the same time in Rome and other places; how, with the usual impetuosity of out-and-out reformers, they confounded the good with the bad, arming themselves with bran-span new brooms wherewith to sweep into the limbo of used-up things the science of Counterpoint, with all its accessories of canon, fugue, imitation, inversion, augmentation, diminution, and a hundred other musical artifices, with a view to putting in its place something or other —they knew not yet exactly what—which they were pleased to call the restored "Musical Declamation of the Greeks."

This attempt of course failed; but the effects which indirectly resulted from it acted on the Musical Art most beneficially. Few experiments were needed to show to these vehement Classicists that they could not get on at all without "Gothic" art; and they were not long in calling to their assistance several professors of that very musical science the destruction of which had seemed to be the first condition of their own success. Among these was Claudio Monteverde—an artist both competent and willing to try his hand at a new style of architecture, but far too well acquainted with the powers of brick and stone to build long with unproved materials. The extent however to which men of sound and commonly sober judgment may be influenced for a time, even in matters of which they are the best possible judges, by ignorant enthusiasm, was never shown more clearly than in the effect at first produced on Monteverde by the Florentine Academy. Not only are many of his first attempts at this Musical Declamation of the Greeks, or "Aria Parlante," dismally dull, but they present examples of grammatical inaccuracy which could not have resulted from ignorance or carelessness, but rather from a determination to throw off all restraint, and show his contempt for the wisdom of his ancestors. This aberration was not however unbroken. At certain moments his early training shows itself, his good genius prevails, and Monteverde is at once correct, tasteful, and original. A fragment of aria parlante* which he has given to the heroine in his opera *Ariadne*, written in 1607 for the Court of Mantua, will sufficiently prove this. Some of the harmonic progressions in it are a little hard ; but the voice part is melodious, and admirably fitted to the sentiment and rhythm of the words. The harmony and melody of the passage " in così dura sorte, in così gran martire" are strikingly expressive and original.

---

* It may not be amiss, once for all, to remind the reader or performer of the following and other similar passages that aria parlante is *not* recitative,—but *melody*, wherein the composer has striven to imitate or embody the accents of impassioned declamation by successions and distributions of notes which, unless literally rendered, *i.e.*, sung *in time*, will be unintelligible and cannot be properly accompanied.

ARIA PARLANTE.—LASCIATE MI MORIR.

From the Opera "*Ariadne.*"   MONTEVERDE.

La-scia - te mi mo - ri - re,   La - scia - te mi mo-

ri - re,   E che vo - le - te voi   che mi con - for - ti

in co-sì du-ra sor-te, in co-sì gran   mar - ti-re? La-

scia - te mi mo-ri - re,   La-scia-te mi   mo - ri - re.

cres.   *f*   *dim.*

The fate of all pioneers has been that of Monteverde. His star has had "to pale" its "ineffectual fire" in the presence of a nearer if not a greater light; and his works have been hidden from the eye of posterity by those of a successor whose powers were not of necessity so much greater, as his opportunities of cultivating them were more favourable. Giacomo Carissimi, whose influence direct and indirect on the history of his art has proved greater perhaps than that of any other master before or since, and whose career occupied the principal part of the seventeenth century, must be regarded as the type and glory of the Transition Period. Strangely enough, in regard to so distinguished a person, the particular years both of Carissimi's birth and death are unknown; but it is certain that he was born not later than 1585, and that he was living in 1672. He might therefore have seen Palestrina; and in all likelihood he lived to hear Corelli. He began life when the "Madrigal" had attained its highest perfection and its greatest favour; he witnessed its decline and extinction. As a contemporary he must have watched the struggle made by the later masters of the Roman School to prolong its moribund existence; he must have been cognizant of the birth and adolescence, though not of the maturity of the Musical Drama; he must have seen Instrumental Music, which he would first have known as a somewhat helpless and very humble dependency, disengage itself from vocal, and assert and make good its claim as an independent and separate power; he must have known—possibly he survived—Stradella, the first great Singer (in the full sense of that misapplied word) of whom we have any definite and trustworthy account; and he was not merely a witness but an instrument of changes in the language of Music such as it has taken five centuries at least to bring about in our own language; for Chaucer and Tennyson have not expressed themselves in a more different idiom than Palestrina and Corelli.

Carissimi, a Paduan by birth, no doubt received his first musical impressions from Venice—always as innovating and aggressive in Art as it was conservative and timid in Politics. At the time he was a youth the Venetian Giovanni Gabrieli was in the full exercise of his powers, and at the summit of his reputation. To him (as we shall see) the subsequently great school of Germany is under heavy obligations; and to him, as the instructor, direct or indirect, of Carissimi, the Italian, the French, and even the English Schools, are no less deeply indebted.

There is not much to be told, even were there time now to tell it, concerning Carissimi's life, long as it certainly was, and busy as it must have been. The best years of it were undoubtedly spent in Rome, where, through his connexion with the disciples of St. Filippo Neri, his attention was turned to that form of musical drama which, from the place in which it was first essayed, the Oratory, took the name of " Oratorio." A considerable number of the very numerous compositions of Carissimi are of this class; that best known by name* is his "Jephtha," one of the choruses of which, with the slightest possible alteration, Handel has paid Carissimi the compliment of inserting bodily in *his* oratorio " Samson." As on a former occasion I gave a specimen of this work, I will call your attention to-day to an extract from another, which I have never seen in a complete form, but which seems to be a sort of " Mystery," concluding with a recitative and trio descriptive of the sufferings of the wicked. You will not fail to remark a considerable advance in this recitative on the specimen by Monteverde which was just given; and those who are familiar with the anthems of Purcell and his contemporaries, who wrote about half a century later, will recognise more than one familiar passage the transmission of which I shall account for in its proper place.

* An edition of it has recently been published in Germany, edited by Chrysander (1876).

RECITATIVO.—TURBABUNTUR IMPII.

CARISSIMI.

Tur - ba - bun-tur im - pi - i ti - mo - re hor - ri - bi - li Cum de-

mf

scen-dent in ter-ram te - ne - bro-sam et o - per-tam, mor-tis ca - li - gi - ne,

U - bi nul - lus or - do, sed sem-pi - ter-nus hor-ror in - ha - bi-

a tempo

tat, præ an - gus - ti - a spi - ri - tus ge - men-tes et di - cen - tes,

TRIO.

un - di-que, un - di-que pa-vor, luc - tus et an - gus - ti-

un - di-que, un - di-que pa-vor, luc - tus et an - gus - ti-

oc - cu-pat, pa-vor, luc - tus et an - gus - ti-

CHORUS.

a, des-pe-ra - vi - mus.

a, des-pe-ra - vi - mus, des-pe-ra - vi - mus.

CHORUS.

a, des-pe-ra - vi-mus, des-pe-ra - vi - mus.

c 2

Quis sta-re po - te-rit cum ig-ne de-vo-ran-te?

Quis sta-re po - te - rit cum ar-

Qua - re non su - mus in u - te - re mor-tu - i?

do - ri-bus sem-pi - ter - nis? Qua - re,

tes, pe - re - at di - es, pe - re - at di - es

tes, pe - re - at di - es, pe - re - at di - es

tes, pe - re - at di - es, pe - re - at di - es, pe - re - at di - es

in qua na - ti su-mus, pe - re - at nox, pe - re - at

in qua na - ti su-mus, pe - re - at nox, pe - re - at, pe - re - at

in qua na - ti su-mus, pe - re - at di - es, pe - re - at, pe - re - at

The influence of Carissimi, either directly by means of personal instruction, or indirectly through the performance and circulation of his compositions, made itself felt (as I have just said) up to very distant and different times, and in very distant and different countries, from those in which he himself lived and worked. Not only so; it affected seriously a class of music to which he never contributed a specimen, Opera; for Carissimi is the connecting link between the generation of which Monteverde is the type and that later and more numerous one of which Cavalli and Cesti are two of the most distinguished representatives.

Francesco Cavalli, born at Venice about the year 1610, began to write for the theatre about 1637, and produced, chiefly in his native city, a succession of works in the course of which he gradually introduced a style of composition superior, as respects musical form consistently with fitness for the scene, to anything that had been employed before on the stage. In his opera " Giasone," first performed in 1649, he would seem to have marked more distinctly than any predecessor the line which separates air from recitative; a line which some of the most recent dramatic composers of our own time, Wagner for instance, and even Gounod, seem to be doing their best to obliterate. An example of one of these very early attempts at dramatic melody will not be without interest to you. It is from the opera " Erismena," produced in 1655. Observe the ingenious manner in which (at *) the first subject is repeated—with a slight change, not only of notes but of rhythm—beginning again, not on the first beat of the bar, but on the second. In the second section of the song a modulation is made into the scale of the dominant quite in the modern manner; but the rest of it is somewhat laboured, showing that Cavalli felt precisely the same difficulty which besets an inexperienced composer of our own time—that of resisting the tendency to modulate into the scale of the subdominant. The addition of the minor seventh to the tonic of any given piece of music is so easy, and the effect of it so pleasing! But, like many other easy and pleasant things, it has to be paid for subsequently by such tiresome and uphill work! A passage (at †) in this second section is striking, as having reappeared many years after in the Psalm tune known as " Hanover," sometimes attributed to Handel. But the most interesting historical peculiarity of the song is that it closes with a repetition of the first strain. This contrivance— the " Da Capo" as it is now called—is often said to have been first resorted to by Alessandro Scarlatti, who was not born till 1659 —four years after the production of the opera from which this song of Cavalli's is taken. Possibly Scarlatti was the first who used it skilfully, which certainly Cavalli has not, in this instance, done. We shall see at our next meeting how much more effective the " Da Capo" became under Scarlatti's treatment.

SONG.—VAGHE STELLE.

From the Opera " *Erismena.*"   1655.   Francesco Cavalli.

Va - ghe stel - le, Lu - ci- bel - le, Non dor - mi - te, non dor - mi - te. Va - ghe stel - le, Lu - ci - bel - le, Non dor - mi - te, non dor - mi - te.

Lu - ci - di sguar - di I lu - mi deh a - pri - te, Deh,

fr

Deh, Lu - ci - di sguar - di I lu - mi, i lu - mi a -

pri - te, Deh lu - ci - di sguar - di i lu - mi, Deh a - pri -

D. C.

te, Bei lu - ci - di sguar - di i lu - mi deh a - pri - te.

D. C.

Marc-Antonio Cesti, another disciple of the school of Carissimi, whose epoch is about ten years later than that of Cavalli, perhaps excelled the latter in his own particular style. Nor was this to be wondered at. Musical execution made such rapid strides during the first half of the seventeenth century that any fairly-taught intelligent musician could produce *effects* which no one would have even contemplated ten years before his time. Monteverde has recorded that, in a passage of accompaniment which he brought forward at Venice in 1624, having, for the first time, substituted sixteen iterated semi-quavers for one semibreve, in several successive bars, the performers one and all refused at first even to try to play them ; so monstrous and extravagant an innovation seemed this now most familiar of instrumental details. Cesti, however, was something more than a fairly-taught intelligent musician ; his invention was of a very high class. He was an Ecclesiastic ; but his orders, whatever their kind, would seem to have hung loosely upon him. He wrote little ecclesiastical music, though he was for many years a member of the choir of the Sistine Chapel. The majority of his numerous compositions were operas, composed nearly all for the theatres of Venice. A duet for Soprano and Bass, *Cara e dolce libertà*, which you will now hear, is a good example of his manner. You would never have supposed, and indeed you will find it hard to believe, that it is two hundred years old. The parts have that easy flow which generally characterizes Italian vocal writing—the earliest hardly less than the most recent, the most superficial no less than the most profound : while they are treated with just enough of contrapuntal artifice to redeem them from the insipidity with which this easy flow is so closely connected. The repetition in the fourth below (at *) of the preceding phrase must have been a novelty in the middle of the seventeenth century, and the re-introduction of the first subject, after this principal and only modulation, is a pleasing example of the art which conceals art.

DUETTO.—CARA E DOLCE LIBERTÀ.

Andantino.

M. A. Cesti.

Ca - ra, ca - ra e dol - ce, Ca - ra, ca - ra, dol - ce, ca - ra e

Ca - ra, ca - ra e dol - ce Li - ber - tà, Ca - ra, dol - ce, ca - ra,

dol - ce Li - ber - tà, ... Ca - ra e dol - ce Li - ber-

ca - ra e dol - ce Li - ber - tà, ... Ca - ra e dol - ce Li - ber-

tà, L'al - mà mia con - so - li tu, Più non vi - vo ser - vi tu, Il mio cor sciol - to sen'

tà, L'al - mà mia con - so - li tu, Più non vi - vo ser - vi tu, Il mio cor sciol - to sen'

Enough has been said to show that the first half of the seventeenth century is an important era in the history of music. Important as it is, however, it yields in importance, if not in interest, to the second half of that century—an era charac-terized not only by the continued and always accelerating development of old forms but by the creation of what may be called a new one.

Up to the end of the sixteenth century Instrumental Music holds so low a place, in comparison with vocal, that it hardly claims serious consideration as a part of musical history. Some of the great masters of the second period—men to whom nothing connected with their art would have been alien or uninteresting—have no doubt left proofs of their versatility, in Variations on some known theme, or "Divisions" on a "Ground," chiefly for the keyed instruments of their time—the precursors of the harpsichord; and some of the best of these which have been preserved are by Englishmen.   But even these very pieces owe their preservation—as indeed most of their interest—to the fact of their being the work of men who were also the authors of vocal music of such intrinsic excellence that it has lost little of its popularity even in the present day.* The mechanical deficiencies, the want of finish, of all musical instruments, up to a comparatively recent time, were alone enough to have checked any progress in instrumental music at all commensurate with that in vocal; and so long as the latter was chiefly choral and (so to speak) self-contained, as there would be little necessity for, so there would be little likelihood of, the former overtaking it. But, with the very first beginnings of the musical drama, the *status* of instrumental music experienced a great and sudden change.   Recitative of necessity required accompaniment, air

---

* *E.g.*—Bird's "Bow Thine Ear," an anthem still all but unrivalled; certainly unsurpassed, in construction, expression, and even effect. Bird (born about 1545) belongs of course to the Elizabethan era, though he lived till the accession of Charles I.

something like interlude or ritornelle; symphony was needed to give force and meaning to pantomime, and dancing in silence is proverbially the most ridiculous of all human transactions. A new direction was at once given to musical and mechanical inventiveness, and the thoughts of many ingenious persons were suddenly turned to the composition of pure instrumental music, to increase of skill in the performance of it, and to improvement in the instruments on which it was to be performed. Of these instruments it would easily be found that incomparably the most important were the Violin family—a family whose origin is lost in the obscurity of pre-historic times, and which up to about the middle of the sixteenth century had remained in too rude and humble a condition to justify any claim to the influence which it subsequently attained. The rapid improvement—or, I should rather say, perfection—of these instruments, due mainly to three Cremonese houses, the Amati, the Guarnerii, and the Straduarii, soon reacted on executive skill; and executive skill is rarely unconnected with ambition, and never long unobserved. From a mere adjunct, rather felt than heard, and tolerated rather than acknowledged, accompaniment began to rival that which it accompanied, in interest and beauty; and, from a dependency or appanage, Instrumental Music grew into an independent and rival power.

This emancipation can hardly be said to have been consummated in Italy till the latter part of the seventeenth century— the epoch of Bassani and Corelli. In England, as we shall see by-and-by, it was brought about some forty years earlier. But, as always proves to be the case in respect to great discoveries, those of Bassani and Corelli had been anticipated, even among their own countrymen,—by one especially who, working with inferior means and appliances, and in less propitious times, had produced a composition which, in the number and relation of its parts, and the instruments by which they are to be played, is still, at the distance of two centuries, a type and a model.

At some time before the year 1650 (he died in 1652) Gregorio Allegri wrote a "Quartetto," for *violini, viola,* and *basso di viola.* Allegri is chiefly known as one of the last of that great Roman School of purely vocal music of which Palestrina is the type and glory. He is the composer of two out of the three settings of the Fiftieth Psalm (the *Miserere*), the performance of which forms so interesting a feature in the music of the Holy Week at Rome. It is the composition which Mozart when a boy (no copy ever having been allowed to be taken) wrote out from memory. As a great master in this style, and the author of perhaps the earliest piece in another which has since attained to such high perfection and favour, Gregorio Allegri may well be considered as the last of the Ancients and the first (in point of time, of course) of the Moderns. Few pieces of music have been honoured by more frequent mention than this quartet. It figures in almost every existing memoir and criticism having relation to the musical history of the seventeenth century. A copy of it has fortunately been preserved in a theoretical work now become rare, and certainly not likely ever to be reprinted, the "Musurgia" of Kircher, published in the year 1650. The obsolete notation and clumsy musical typography of this work must have rendered the performance of any of the examples it contains all but impossible for at least a hundred and fifty years past; and it is probable that the piece in question never found performers or audience, even during the last century; far less can it have done so in this. Thanks to the co-operation of four of my professional friends, you will in a few minutes be in a position to form an estimate of it. I need hardly warn you not to expect anything like any quartet you are likely to hear at the Musical Union or anywhere else. And you will forgive me for entreating you, once for all, to listen to this and other pieces of the same epoch, not with nineteenth, but with seventeenth-century ears. No one would think of complaining that Giotto was not Rubens, or Chaucer not Pope; so you will not be disappointed in finding that Allegri is not Mendelssohn.

The work consists of four movements, all of them in the contrapuntal and fugued style. The first movement is on two subjects, the second of which is introduced by the viola, in the 15th bar. The second movement is in triple time, and opens with a very pretty phrase of six bars, the bass part of which is afterwards made the subject of a second fugue—in the old sense of that word. This passes without interruption into a third movement on a new subject in "alla capella" or duple time. The fourth and concluding movement is in common time and on a subject admitting of exceedingly close "imitation."

The composition* presents an interesting example of uncertain tonality—oscillating as it does (to a modern musical ear) between the keys of G and of C,—the forms of the passages inclining us towards G, and the frequent recurrence of F natural bringing us back again to C. It ends with a perfect cadence in G, so brought about as to have the effect rather of a modulation preparatory to a fresh movement than of a close.

---

* Its length has prevented its insertion here *entire;* but the Andante— the second and most pleasing movement—will give an idea at least of the character of the work. The entries of the different instruments are severally indicated by 1 and 2, 1st and 2nd Violins, V, Viola, and B, Basso.

ANDANTE FROM A QUARTET.

GREGORIO ALLEGRI.

LECTURE II.

ITALY—CONTINUED.

CHANGE OF TONALITY—SUBDIVISION IN MUSICAL FORMS—
SINGING—STRADELLA—PISTOCCHI—SCHOOL OF BOLOGNA
—CHAMBER MUSIC—MARCELLO—SALMO XXV.—CLARI—
DUETTO, "QUANDO TRAMONTA IL SOLE"—ALESSANDRO
SCARLATTI—ARIA, "LASCIAMI PIANGERE"—THE NEAPO-
LITAN SCHOOL—DURANTE—HIS PUPILS—QUARTET, "RE-
GINA ANGELORUM"—PERGOLESI—HIS "STABAT MATER."

LECTURE II.

ITALY—CONTINUED.

I OBSERVED in my last lecture, in reference to the Old Masters, that there was "no want of that general accordance between the style of their music and the sentiments of the words to which it is set which is the first condition of musical expression," but that " this accordance was never more than general ;" and that nothing "like that close following in music of the various changes of feeling expressed in poetry to which we moderns are habituated had ever suggested itself to a composer of the second period." Indeed, the conditions both of the science and the art of music down to about the end of the sixteenth century rendered it all but impossible that any attempt at this " close following" of words by notes could have been successful, even had it ever been made.

But, as we have seen, about the beginning of the seventeenth century the particular tonality, or scale system, which had so long prevailed in the schools, began to give place to another, the subsequent universal adoption of which has resulted in the production of music altogether without precedent, whether for expression or any other quality, the music of the Fourth Period —the period of Mozart and Beethoven.

During the whole of the century on which our attention has been so far fixed (the seventeenth) musical science and musical art may be said to have been engaged in an unintermittent struggle with the causes that had so long prevented their perfect union—the falseness of the former and the rudeness of the latter. But by about the end of that century—so far as we can trace its progress in the best of all historical records, monuments—musical science succeeded in working its way towards a solid and enduring basis; musical art borrowing from it or lending to it, as its occasional weakness, but on the whole ever-increasing strength, enabled it to do. With the science we have now no further concern than as it can be shown to have acted directly on the art, which began now to show the most decisive of all signs of development—a tendency to subdivision in its forms. We have already had occasion to notice several of these; the musical drama, sacred and secular, the cantata, and—perhaps a still greater advance on anything done before—various kinds of music for instruments only. These different and continually developing forms of composition exacted of course corresponding varieties and improvements in musical performance, and among these in singing. Singing is possibly the oldest of musical arts, and, as it might be supposed, the first which would attain perfection. As of all powers which die with their owners, it is impossible to arrive at any satisfactory estimate of the condition of the art of singing at any very distant period. We may safely assume that at all times there have been persons of strong and deep feeling and fine musical instincts, who have been also gifted with beautiful voices; and that these persons, in some way or other, succeeded in making their ways to the hearts of their hearers. It would seem, however, that singing only began to deserve the name of an art as late as the middle of the seventeenth century. Singing implies not merely voice, sentiment and musical knowledge but training of a very especial kind, to enable the possessors of these to turn them to account. And it is not till about this time that we hear anything of such training, or of any individual performers whose vocal powers were at all distinguished. A vast number of persons must have been able, even early in the sixteenth century, to sing by no means easy music, from book, in tune and in time. In England especially the number of vocalists must have been then very great indeed. But this music was not of a kind to call for very high finish in its performance; and those who took part in it did so more often for their own pleasure than for that of any listeners; just, in fact, as people dance now —well or ill, as the case may be, but equally to their own satisfaction and enjoyment. Vocal skill of this kind and degree, however, is not what is or should be understood by singing, which, I repeat, is an art the invention or it may be revival of which is not yet two centuries old. For, the first vocal performer in modern times of whom we have any account which will justify our believing him to have been what we should now call a singer, was Alessandro Stradella, no less celebrated as a composer than as a performer, and still better known to the world on account of the touching story of his life and death— a story so strange as well as touching that we should find it hard to believe it to be true, did we not know that truth *is* strange—stranger than fiction.

To tell this story in a few words would be impossible, and for long stories, however interesting in themselves, we have no time. Besides, it may be found, with some varieties of detail, but in its essential particulars identical, in almost every existing work which treats of musical history and biography. It does not appear that Stradella communicated any of the secrets of his art to others, or that he formed any distinguished pupils. Still less, during his short career, could he have organized anything like a school. Nor indeed was any such organization attempted till about the end of the century in which he flourished, when Francesco Pistocchi (b. 1659), an excellent musician, who had failed as a dramatic singer, probably from insufficient physical power, established an academy at Bologna, in which many of the best Italian singers of the early part of the last century were educated, and which was the model of the numerous other academies which soon after sprang up in other Italian cities, especially Naples. In the Bolognese academy founded by

Pistocchi singing was first taught systematically; *i.e.*, to the study of musical grammar, composition, and generally the practice of some instrument, was added instruction in the mechanical part of the singer's art—" production" or delivery of voice, management of breath, "vocalization," pronunciation, carriage of the body, and (what we have such high authority for the importance of, to those who would affect others) action. How efficient this instruction must have been, and what apt scholars they were who received it is well known. During the eighteenth century Italy was, above all others, the Land of Song, and Italian opera the recreation, I had almost said the passion, of the whole civilized world.

Although musical expression owes more to the musical drama —under which head I include oratorio as well as opera—than to any other form of composition, composers of other kinds of music were not unmindful of its importance. Vocal chamber music, after the madrigal had declined in public favour, took various new forms, in connexion with sacred as well as with secular poetry.

The most distinguished composer of sacred chamber music— *i.e.*, music neither dramatic nor ecclesiastical—of the early part of the last century, was the Venetian Benedetto Marcello, born in 1786. This noble and in every sense distinguished amateur was, as we learn from contemporary testimony, a man of very varied powers and accomplishments, which he brought to bear on equally various occupations. He filled a succession of political offices conformable to his rank : he was a member of the Council of Forty, and acted on more than one occasion both as an ambassador and a provincial governor. He would seem to have been a linguist above even Venetian average, having attained some reputation for his knowledge of Hebrew. But what chiefly concerns us at this moment is that he was a voluminous writer of and about music, a composer of oratorios, operas, and instrumental music, and the author of numerous treatises, pamphlets, and satirical pieces relating to the musical art his passion for which even led him in several instances to act as a singing master. The celebrated Faustina, afterwards Madame Hasse, whose subsequent rivalry with Cuzzoni, during her stay in London, forms so amusing an episode in the life of Handel, was for a time his pupil. The musical work by which Marcello is best known is his setting of Giustiniani's paraphrase of the first fifty Psalms of David. Few have attained wider celebrity, nor is there any one of equal bulk (it extends to eight folio volumes) of which reprints have been more numerous. Among these tributes of admiration not the least hearty is the English adaptation projected by Avison of Newcastle, but subsequently carried into effect by Garth of Durham. Nor has favourable criticism been wanting to swell the fame of Marcello's Psalms. The Venetian edition of Sebastiano Valle, published in 1803, is prefaced by a highly encomiastic memoir, and accompanied by numerous laudatory epistles and a collection of " testimonianze," the sincerity of which, the reader is told, cannot be questioned, since they were all written after the death of the subject of them. The style of the memoir may be judged of from one extract. " In respect to the title of ' Principe di Musica,' that has been awarded to Marcello, no one competent to form a judgment on such matters can doubt that he fully deserved it." Marcello died in 1733, when—not to speak of his compatriots of the preceding century, or of his German contemporaries, Handel and J. S. Bach —Scarlatti, Vinci, Leo, Durante, and Pergolesi had produced the majority of their best compositions.

The judgment of posterity has not quite confirmed that of Marcello's contemporaries. The cause of this is not far to seek. Throughout the work the frequent and sudden changes of sentiment in the text are followed by the music with a pertinacity often not merely injurious to the effect of the latter but even inconsistent with anything like good musical construction. In his determination to carry musical expression as far as he could, Marcello has sometimes carried it too far, and in taxing its powers to the utmost he has occasionally overtaxed them. A sense of weariness comes over the most patient performer, reader, or hearer who is long kept under the influence of Marcello's psalmody ; and this not from the length, but from the shortness, of the individual movements. This incessant coming to an end and beginning again is no doubt to be defended on the score of the abrupt, fragmentary, or fitful character of the Psalms themselves; but it may be questioned whether, with Marcello, it was not a result as much of necessity as of choice, and whether he has not availed himself of this restless variety in order to hide that deficiency of constructive skill which the works of so many composers of the third period betray. Granting this however, Marcello's Psalms remain a most remarkable monument of invention and taste ; nor does there perhaps exist a musical work from which so many individual passages could be detached which would obtain more hearty and general admiration.

Every variety to be created by purely vocal resources is adopted in Marcello's Psalms. We find often, at very short intervals, recitative, aria parlante, and air, for a single voice ; movements for two, three, four, and five solo voices—these grouped in the most original ways, and varied and reinforced by choral parts. Some of these movements still keep their places in popular collections of sacred music, and even find their way from time to time into concert programmes—The Duet " Qual anelante" for instance, and the Solo and Chorus "I cieli immensi narrano." On the present occasion I shall call your attention to the first movement of Marcello's setting of the Twenty-fifth Psalm, which will probably be new to most of you. The interest of the vocal part (for a contralto voice) is greatly increased by the addition and support of a violoncello accompaniment.

SALMO XXV.

MARCELLO.

te, che m'as - sal d'og-n' in - tor - no deh pie - to - so mi

sal - va, mi . . sal - va poi-chè in te so - lo og - ni mia

spe-me è pos - ta.

Ho sem-pre det-to: il mio Sig - nor tu

se - i, tu se - i per che' il ret - to oprar mi - o

di tua de - men-za è . . . do - no,

e pur d'uo-po non hai, non

hai pro - fit - to del-le ret - te, o - pre

mi - e,   d'uo-po non ha - i,   non hai pro-

fit - to del-le ret - te o - pre   mi - e.

Marcello and some of his contemporaries must have owed much to a musician born about twenty years earlier than they (in 1669), the Abbate Clari. The name and works of Clari, comparatively forgotten and neglected during the greater part of the last century, have recently been brought a good deal into notice. Very little more has been recorded about his personal history than that he was a Pisan by birth, studied under Giovanni Paolo Colonna at Bologna, and became subsequently Chapel-master in the cathedral of Pistoia. He does not appear to have been a very prolific writer; but that he was a very inventive, tasteful, and scientific one is happily easily ascertained. In the well-known volumes published by the late Mr. Novello under the title of " Fitzwilliam Music" there are many of Clari's compositions, more especially some extracts from a " Stabat Mater," which, if they are fair specimens, would show Clari's setting of that Hymn to deserve a high place among the many which have come down to us. Clari's reputation however is chiefly due to his " Madrigali o Duetti." These, besides exhibiting some technical excellences which must have been novelties at the time of their production, may be regarded as some of the earliest secular vocal music which could be called both elegant and learned; for, with a freedom, and even where required a playfulness, that might become the least pretentious and most ephemeral of contemporary sketches, they combine almost every contrapuntal artifice which would be called into requisition in the most ambitious and lasting work. One of these duets, " Cantando un dì," revived first I believe in Choron's Singing School in Paris some thirty-five or forty years since, has subsequently gone the round of all musical Europe. For some years no concert programme seemed complete without it, and it is still much sung by intelligent amateurs. As this duet is perfectly accessible I prefer introducing you to another, more especially as it involves a combination of voices, Soprano and Tenor, less likely to be often at hand than those for which " Cantando un dì" is written, two Sopranos.

DUETTO.—QUANDO TRAMONTA IL SOLE.

Un poco lento. (♩ = 80.)   CLARI.

Quan - do tra - mon - ta il so - le, Và   can - tan do o-gni au-

gel - lo, Và can - tan - do, can - tan - do o-gni au-gel - lo,

Quan - do tra - mon - ta il so - le, Và   can - tan - do o-gni au-

Al ni - do, al - ni - do om - bro - so,

gel - lo, Al ni - do, al ni - do om - bro - so, Quan - do tra-

Quan - do tra-mon-ta il so - le, Quan - do tra-

po - so, Và can - tan - do o-gn'au-gel-lo,

mon - ta il so-le, Và can - tan - do ogn'au-

Và can - tan - do, can - tan - do ogn'au-gel - lo, E

gel - lo, E lie - ta Ni - gel - la

lie - ta - Ni - gel - la ri - con-

ri - con - dar, ri - con - dar l'a - gnel - - le suo -

dar, ri - con - dar l'a - gnel - - - le suo -

le, Và can - tan - d'ogni au - gel - lo, Và can -

le, Quan - do tra - mon - ta il so-le, Quan - do tra-mon - ta il

tan - do ogn'au - gel - lo, ogn'au - gel - lo, E lie - -

so - le, Và can - tan - do ogn' au gel -lo, E

I have now to speak of a musician whose influence on his art may be clearly traced down to our own time, but whose compositions have entirely passed from that public favour of which they once enjoyed so large a share, and of whose life so little is generally known that he is often confounded with his own son, an able and interesting person without doubt, but altogether less able and less interesting than his father.

No one who has looked at all into the history of music and the biography of musicians can have failed to notice that the greatest composers have been the most prolific. We have no "single speech Hamiltons," no Giorgiones who have left a few specimens only of a talent hardly inferior to that of the greatest of their fellows. Palestrina, Carissimi, Handel, Bach, Haydn, Mozart, Beethoven, Mendelssohn, have done not only better but more than other musicians. Measured by this rule Alessandro Scarlatti is justly entitled to a place in the illustrious company I have named, for he was the composer of certainly one hundred and twelve operas, perhaps more, of at least two hundred masses, of eight or ten oratorios, of an immense number of sacred cántatas, hymns, psalms, motets, and other church music, and of detached pieces—madrigals, duets, and songs, with and without accompaniment—the most moderate estimate of the number of which would be at first received with utter incredulity. Nor let it be for a moment imagined that the majority of these were in any sense what are called slight works. Many of them no doubt are slightly accompanied; the single songs for example, most of which have merely a figured bass; but others, on the contrary, are scored with great skill, none the less great because the instruments employed are few in number. As for his concerted vocal music, especially what are somewhat loosely called his Madrigals, they are elaborated perhaps to excess. One of these, the madrigal " Cor mio," written for four sopranos and a contralto, which has been preserved in the " Saggio del Contrapunto" of Martini, who has accompanied it by a careful analysis, is unquestionably one of the most learned pieces of music in existence.

But these productions, enough of themselves, and more than enough, to have occupied the whole of the lives of half-a-dozen musicians of average talent and industry, would seem to have been the recreations of Scarlatti. The *work* of his life was the founding and the raising of what has since been known as the School of Naples, in which were educated nearly all the most eminent Italian composers of the last century, and the majority of those extraordinary vocalists—*e.g.,* Faustina, La Gabrielli, Mingotti, Senesino, Bernacchi, Cafarelli, Guadagni, Pacchie- rotti, Marchesi, and Farinelli—whose lives, the ephemeral nature of their talent notwithstanding, have become a part of the history of their time. Nor is this all. The *in*direct influence of Scarlatti, through this school, was even more im- portant than the direct; for (as I hope to show at the right time) the particular direction which the genius and scholarship of Handel eventually took, is mainly due to his visit to Italy and his intercourse, for three years, with Scarlatti and his pupils. It cannot be questioned that but for this visit and this inter- course Handel's music would have been—no one can say what, but—assuredly very different music to what it turned out to be.

We have time for only one specimen of Alessandro Scarlatti's talent, but it is a characteristic specimen, the harmony rich and varied, and the melody large, flowing, and admirably expressive of the words, which, like those of all the songs of this epoch, are limited to two or three lines rather indicating than exhausting a single thought. I do not know whether the air which you will now hear forms part of any one of Scarlatti's numerous operas. I should think not. I found it in a MS. volume of Cantatas, chiefly by him, which came into my possession a short time since.

ARIA.—LASCIAMI PIANGERE.

Lento non troppo. (♩ = 60.)   ALESSANDRO SCARLATTI.

La - scia-mi, la - scia-mi pian - ge - re ch'io sò per-

chè io sò, io sò, io sò per-chè.

La - scia-mi pian - ge-re,

la - scia-mi pian - ge-re ch'io sò per-chè, per-chè, ch'io sò per-

chè, La - scia-mi pian - ge - re ch'io sò per - chè, io

sò, io sò, io sò per - chè.

Del-le mie la - gri-me La sor - te

per - fi - da Sa - zia non è, sa - zia non è.

Del-le mie la-gri-me La sor-te per-fi-da Sa-zia non

è, Del-le mie la-gri-me La sor-te per-fi-da

Sa-zia non è nò, nò, nò nò, nò, sa - - zia non

Da Capo.

è. La-scia-mi

p *f*

It is of course impossible for me to speak in detail of all the musicians educated in the Neapolitan School who successively rose to eminence as composers, conductors, vocal or instrumental performers, or teachers. Simply to name them would be useless and uninteresting. I will ask you to devote what little time remains to us to two of these, Durante and Pergolesi; types, the former of the learning, the latter of the genius, of their epoch and country.

Francesco Durante was born in Naples in 1693. At an early age he came under the notice of Scarlatti, and received instruction from him for some years. Subsequently he visited Rome, where he studied singing under Petroni and counterpoint under Pasquini. On his return to his native city he soon attracted attention by his broad and scientific style of composition, and at the age of twenty-two obtained a position in the Conservatory of S. Onofrio, soon after which he was appointed Chapel-master in the Conservatory Dei Poveri di Giesù Christo. This institution having been converted by the Archbishop of Naples into an ecclesiastical college, Durante, deprived of his regular occupation, became for a time dependent for subsistence on his pen. To this period, extending over five years, must be assigned the majority of the compositions to which he owes his fame. On the death of Leo, in 1745, he returned to his old quarters in S. Onofrio, in the capacity of musical director. To the discharge of the duties of this office the remaining ten years of his life were devoted. He died, aged 62, in 1755.

Durante was one of those artists who should be estimated as much by their personal influence as by what they leave behind them in a tangible or appreciable form. Personal influence is not susceptible of any very exact measurement, and the amount of Durante's must to a great extent be taken on trust. Something may be gathered from the fact that—not to speak of what many musicians whose names have not come down to us, and the society in which he lived, owed to him—Durante was the instructor during his first professorship (in the Conservatory Dei Poveri di Giesù Christo) of Pergolesi, Duni, Traetta, Vinci, Terradeglias, and Jomelli; and during the second (in the Conservatory of S. Onofrio) of Piccinni, Sacchini, Guglielmi and Paisiello.

But in his own day Durante was hardly less esteemed as a composer than as a teacher. He still stands high; he deserves perhaps to stand higher. His views of the dignity of his art must have been lofty, not to say severe. He never wrote for the Theatre, and the only secular works (I believe) which bear his name are a collection of Chamber Duets, not of his own composition, but arranged by him, from certain cantatas by his master Scarlatti, as studies for part-singing. Manuscript copies of this collection are not rare, but, strange to say, it has never been printed, although few works have received more frequent or more honourable mention from musical historians and critics.

In the Library of the Paris Conservatoire de Musique there is a large, and probably complete, collection of the compositions of Durante. The catalogue of this, as given by M. Fétis, is a long one, and includes many Masses and other large works, each of necessity consisting of many movements, the majority of which are doubtless considerably developed. Durante is perhaps more remarkable for his treatment of subjects than his invention of them; though the elegance of his part-writing, his skill in instrumentation and, more than all, the sustained dignity of his style, make large amends for the want of inventiveness sometimes complained of in his music.

The composition you will now hear, from a Litany to the Blessed Virgin—one of many which he wrote—is no less remarkable for the originality of its plan than the refinement of its detail. The antiphonal effect with which it starts is maintained throughout, the " prex" being invariably assigned to one voice and the " response" to others.

F

REGINA ANGELORUM.

Durante.

pro - phe - ta - rum,

pro - phe - ta - rum,

pro - phe - ta - rum,

O - ra pro no - bis!

Re - gi - na a - pos - to - lo - rum,

Re - gi - na a - pos - to - lo - rum,

Re - gi - na a - pos - to - lo - rum,

O-

om-ni-um. O - ra pro no - bis!

om-ni-um. O-ra pro no - bis! O - ra pro no-

om-ni-um. O-ra pro no - bis! O-ra pro no -

om-ni-um. O-ra pro no - bis! O-ra pro no -

O - ra pro no - - bis!

bis! O - ra pro no - bis!

bis! O - ra pro no - bis!

bis! O - ra pro no - bis!

But if Durante merit our esteem as the author of this and a hundred other compositions doubtless as interesting, he will have a still stronger claim upon it as the teacher of Pergolesi, a musician whose genius, whose peculiarities—nay, whose very faults—mark him out, among great, and in some respects greater contemporaries, as the type of the Neapolitan Era.

Giovanni Battista Jeri was surnamed *Pergolesi* from the place of his birth, Pergola, a small town in the duchy of Urbino, not far from Pesaro, where, in later times, a still more distinguished, if not more excellent musician, Rossini, first saw the light.

Though more particulars of the life of Pergolesi have been recorded than of the majority of the men of genius who have lived in any but very recent times, the first fact to be mentioned in every biography, the year of his birth, and the last, the year of his death, are both of them matters of uncertainty or dispute. Some of his biographers state the former to have been 1704, some 1707, and some 1710; some give to the latter the date 1737, some 1739. The matter is not so unimportant as it appears. Our estimate of a very long career may not be seriously affected by the addition or subtraction of a very few years, but assuredly it would be satisfactory to know whether the prodigious quantity of music—generally beautiful and always highly finished—which Pergolesi has left behind him was the product of a life of thirty-two years or of only twenty-six. Either way, however, his career is one of the most astonishing recorded in musical history. The list of his works presents examples of every kind of music practised in his day, of oratorios, operas, instrumental chamber music, and above all in number and excellence, of masses, motets, psalms, and hymns. The fate of his operas is remarkable. He wrote in all certainly seven, and perhaps more, only one of which attained any success—so long as success could have contributed to his happiness and worldly prosperity. But no sooner had Death ended (so prematurely) his laborious and somewhat sad career, than the very works which on their first production had met with nothing but indifference or contempt, became the objects of the most passionate admiration, first of his own countrymen and then of all Europe. For some years, whether in the Theatre, in the Concert Room, or in the Church, no music, it is said, was tolerated in Italy but Pergolesi's. His operas, however, like most of the operas of the first half of the last century, are entirely forgotten. Equally as a matter of course his purely instrumental music has shared the same fate. But his church music, and more especially two of his latest works, his "Stabat Mater" and his "Salve Regina," still continue to find occasional hearers, fit though, it may be, few.

The "Stabat Mater" is a hymn of ten stanzas of six lines each, written probably in the thirteenth century, wherein are very touchingly and vividly depicted the sorrows of the Blessed Virgin on the death of our Lord. Its felicitous and, perhaps more, its varied expression have made it a favourite subject among musicians, especially those of Roman Catholic countries. Indeed, there are few of any eminence who have not set portions of it to music. In the fifteenth century it exercised the invention of Josquin Deprès, in the sixteenth that of Palestrina, in the seventeenth that of Clari, in the eighteenth that of Haydn, and in our own time that of Rossini.

But, as a whole, this setting of Pergolesi seems to me equal in most respects, and superior in many, to any of those I have named. I wish there were time for you to hear it as a whole, for every movement of a great work suffers (the finest movements most) in being separated from what comes before and after it. Still, whether as a link in a chain or a fragment out of one, beautiful handiwork is always admirable; and you will I am sure agree with me in thinking that the passage which will now be submitted to you, even torn from its context, is beautiful in itself and a very perfect example of musical expression.

SOLO.—VIDIT SUUM DULCEM NATUM.

From a " *Stabat Mater.*"   Pergolesi.

Tempo Giusto.   (♪ = 108.)

na - tum, Mo - ri - en - tem, de - so - la - tum, Mo - ri -

en - tem, de - so - la - tum, Dum e - mi -

sit spi - ri - tum.

Vi - dit su - um

la - tum, de - so - la - tum, Dum e -

mi - sit, dum e - mi - sit . spi - ri

tum.

LECTURE III.

FRANCE.

THE GALLO-BELGIAN SCHOOL—MERSENNE—THE AGE OF
LOUIS XIII.—DUMONT—METRICAL PSALM, "PEUPLES,
RACONTEZ"—LULLY—SCENE,"J'AI PERDU LA BEAUTÉ"—
AIR, "ROLAND, COUREZ"—COUPERIN—SOLO, "LA VO-
LUPTUEUSE"—RAMEAU—THEORETICAL WRITINGS—
QUARTET, "TENDRE AMOUR"—J. J. ROUSSEAU—WRIT-
INGS ON MUSIC—LE DEVIN AU VILLAGE—LES CONSOLA-
TIONS DES MISÈRES DE MA VIE—AIRS, "JE L'AI PLANTÉ,"
"QUE LE JOUR ME DURE."

LECTURE III.

FRANCE.

I AM under the necessity of alluding again, and of apologizing again for alluding, to my former course of lectures delivered here. During those lectures, I called attention repeatedly to the fact that modern music owed its development chiefly to three peoples—the Gallo-Belgians, the Italians, and the Germans. The majority of French writers on music generally speak of the first of these musical peoples (I have named them in chronological order) as Frenchmen; and the majority of German writers speak of them as Belgians. But, as I have already explained, these exclusive designations are both inappropriate and misleading. Seeing (1) that, although certain persons who might *now* be correctly described as Frenchmen, and certain others who might, with equal propriety, be called Belgians, contributed to form this earliest of modern schools, the frontier line of France and Belgium has, during the last five centuries, been repeatedly changed; and (2) that the birthplaces of many northern musicians of the fifteenth and sixteenth centuries are still unascertained. Moreover, the French school proper, which dates no further back than the middle of the seventeenth century, is not a direct consequence or outgrowth of what I have called the Gallo-Belgian school. This latter came to end, as an individual or independent school, quite within the sixteenth century, Orlando Lasso (properly Roland de Lattre) having died at a very advanced age in 1594. During the first half of the following century (the seventeenth) the history of French music is a blank, only relieved, if relieved it

G

may be said to be, by the writings of a theorist, unquestionably of great ingenuity and still greater industry. This was the Père Mersenne, who early in life took orders as a " Minim" (the Minims were an offshoot of the Franciscans), and devoted his leisure, or more properly his whole time, to the collection of facts bearing on the theory of music, and to speculations growing out of them. He lived, certainly under no very strict monastic rule, in Paris, the friend and associate of the celebrated Descartes. Mersenne would seem to have been the first to call attention to a very important principle in the theory of music,—that the sounds most consonant with one another are those between which the simplest relations, or intervals, exist. *E.g.,* Two sounds an octave apart stand in the relation of 1 : 2, whereas (to take an extreme case) two sounds a major seventh apart stand in the relation of 8 : 15. Many conclusions to which, with better opportunities of investigation, men of science have since arrived, are said to have been anticipated by Mersenne. One in particular* respecting the tension of strings, is noticed by M. Fétis as having been reached by the altogether independent investigation of M. Savart. But these and other of the more useful remarks and more sober speculations of Mersenne are mixed up with statements and propositions indicating such a large amount of credulity and such a small amount of common sense, that the former have now little chance of ever being separated again from the latter. For example, he considers gravely, and at some length, whether the temperament of a "perfect" musician should be sanguine or phlegmatic, bilious or melancholy, in order that he may be best able to sing or compose the most beautiful melodies ; and even what should be the relative positions of the stars at the moment of his birth. Moreover, he seems to have

---

* To raise a string the tension of which is equal to 1 lb. to its octave, a tension equal to 4 lbs. is *not* (as might have been expected) sufficient. It it is necessary to add $\frac{1}{4}$ of lb., *i.e.*, $\frac{1}{16}$ of the whole weight.

been tormented by an indomitable inclination to wander from the subject on which, for the time, he is professedly treating; carrying his reader off, in every other sentence, at a tangent, and offering some new and often irrelevant topic for his consideration.

The writings of Mersenne are voluminous, but the majority of his theories and discoveries are resumed in a work he published in 1636, under the title of " Harmonie Universelle." Even a more useful and interesting book of the same magnitude would hardly find many readers in the present day ; and the curiosity of most of you will be satisfied with the statement that the " Harmonie Universelle" is a closely printed folio of 1500 pages. Mersenne died in 1648, at the age of seventy.

Of music during the reign of Louis XIII. a few names, for the most part of performers on the organ and the clavecin, which have been preserved from utter oblivion in French musical histories, are the only traces. Nor can the long reign of his successor be regarded as one of the epochs of musical history, however remarkable in other respects. Three musicians only can be said to have added anything to the glories of the age of Louis XIV.—Lully, Couperin, and Rameau; and their influence even (unlike that of other really great musicians) hardly extended, save indirectly, beyond the country in which it was first exercised. Yet that in their several ways they were gifted men, and men who had cultivated their gifts, no one who has looked into their works or their biographies would think of questioning. But before bringing this triumvirate under your more especial notice, I must introduce you to a composition by a contemporary musician of smaller calibre and much inferior reputation, an incident in whose life shows his master Louis XIV. in a very amiable light.

Henri Dumont, though a Belgian by birth, was by education and residence a Frenchman. Early in his career (he was born

2

in 1610) he attracted the attention of the King, and was appointed by him musical director of both the Chapels Royal. During the first years of his reign his majesty was content with a choir composed of singers, accompanied only, if at all, by the organ. But the style of church music introduced by Carissimi and his imitators, in Italy, which involved the employment of other instruments, spread so rapidly and so widely, that by the middle of the seventeenth century the Sistine Chapel was almost the only one of note from which they were excluded. Louis XIV. was not likely to be slow in adopting any practice which might add, or seem to add, to the dignity of anything in which he was concerned; and about the year 1670 he desired Dumont to make arrangements for the addition of an orchestra to the appointments of the royal choir. Dumont, now somewhat advanced in life, and perhaps a little diffident of his instrumental knowledge, pleaded one of the decrees of the Council of Trent, wherein the employment of the harp, sackbut, psaltery, and other kinds of instruments was, or seemed to be, prohibited. On this the King, respecting the scruple of his chapel-master, and unwilling to employ authority where persuasion might suffice, consulted Harley, then Archbishop of Paris, on the matter. The Archbishop decided that the intention of the Council had never been to prohibit the use of instrumental music in Divine worship, but only the abuse of it. Dumont still protesting, the King, a short time after, released him from further care about the duties, allowing him still to retain the emoluments of his office.

The composition you will now hear is a very simple one. It is a metrical psalm set, in a somewhat free style, for four voices. The melody, which is striking and graceful, is I presume, like the other parts, by Dumont. I scored it many years ago from a set of old French part-books which were lent to me by the late Dr. Barrett.

LAUDATE PUERI DOMINUM.

Ps. 112

Henri Dumont.

Peu - ples ra - con - tez les lou - an - ges Du Dieu dont

le pou-voir a ba - ti l'U - ni-vers; Et que son nom, si

doux, si doux   En la bou - che   des   an - ges,

doux, si doux   En   la bou - che   des an - ges,

doux, si doux   En   la bou - che des an - ges,

doux, si doux En   la   bou - che   des   an - ges,

Soit l'u - ni - que   su - jet   que cé - lè - brent vos vers.

Soit   l'u - ni - que   su - jet   que   cé - lè - brent   vos vers.

Soit   l'u - ni - que   su - jet   que cé - lè - brent   vos vers.

Des ber - gers fait sou-vent des prin - ces et des rois,

Des ber-gers fait sou-vent des prin - ces et des rois,

Des ber-gers fait sou-vent des prin - ces et des rois,

Des ber-gers fait sou-vent des prin - ces et des rois.

Des ber-gers fait sou-vent des prin - ces et des rois.

Des ber - gers fait sou - vent des prin - ces et des rois.

Des ber-gers fait sou-vent des prin - ces et des rois.

But of far greater interest in every way than Dumont are the
three musicians whom I just now named, and of these again
the most interesting, to us English especially, is Lully; since
(as we shall see by-and-by) through him the Italian style of the
second period, with all that belongs to it, made its way into our
own country.

John Baptist Lully, like Dumont, was not a Frenchman by
birth.   He was born, in the year 1633, at or near Florence:
he even made acquaintance with the elements of music before
he left Italy; for an old monk is said to have taught him to
play upon the guitar.   At the age of thirteen he was carried by
the Chevalier de Guise into France, and placed in the establishment of Madlle. de Montpensier, who, being possessed with a
fine lady's whim to have an Italian page, had commissioned
the Chevalier to bring her one.   Here, his musical talent or
promise being accidentally revealed, he was placed, through the
instrumentality of the Princess, under instruction—of whom is
not recorded.   His progress as a violin player and, in some
small way even, as a composer, soon began to attract attention;
but he was eventually dismissed from a post that had been
given him in the private band of his benefactress, in consequence of his having set to music a gross and indecent libel
upon her. This was but a foretaste of Lully's way of life,
which—it is grievous to have to say this of a man of
genius—proved to be the vilest and coarsest conceivable.
His morals and manners, however, do not seem to have stood
much in the way of his worldly prosperity; at any rate, his
genius balanced any disadvantage to which they might have
put him.   He procured admission into the famous band of
violins—the prototype of the " four-and-twenty fiddlers all of a
row" whom our Charles II. subsequently organized in England;
he found favour with the King, the Princes, and a number of
the nobility, and by command of the King formed a second
orchestra, called " les petits violons," to distinguish them from

the first, who were known as " la grande bande." For these
he wrote an immense number of pieces made up of dance tunes
—sarabands, courants, gigues, &c.—most of which, it is said,
are extant, though still in MS. He composed music also for the
majority of the Court ballets, in which, as is well known, the
highest personages of the realm, even the King himself, took
part. In the year 1664 he struck up an alliance with Molière,
and from that time wrote the incidental music to all his plays.
Nor did he allow even this large amount of professional occupation to absorb his whole time, or to prevent his cultivating or
exercising any faculty that would bring him favour, influence
or money,—for Lully added avarice to the number of his vices.
Like the latter, his talents were certainly very various. For
some years he danced in the Court ballets under the name of
Baptiste, not assuming his patronymic till he had made some
position in the world. Later, however, Molière, persuaded him to
return to the stage, in the new capacity of a low comedian. He
played the part of the "Mufti" in "Le Bourgeois Gentilhomme,"
with great success ; and having displeased the King by some
outrage on propriety too gross or too overt to be ignored, he
restored himself to favour by his performance of " Monsieur de
Pourceaugnac," in the comedy of that name.

To his other gifts Lully added a vein of wit, none the less
abundant or effective for his utter disregard of time, place, or
person in the exercise of it. He may be said to have carried
impudence to a pitch of the sublime ; for he more than once
took a liberty with the Grand Monarque. On the occasion of
a performance at Court, the commencement was, from some
cause, so long delayed that the King sent word to him that he
was tired of waiting. " Le roi est bien le maître," said he,
" il peut s'ennuyer tant qu'il lui plaira." His wit, or in this
case rather his humour, sometimes took the form of a grim
practical joke. Once, during a fit of illness, he sent for a con-
fessor, who, as a condition to granting him absolution, insisted

on his destroying the score of the last opera which he had composed, "Armide," then in rehearsal. The Prince of Conti called to see him the same day, and hearing what had been done, said to him,—" Why, Baptiste, how could you be so foolish as to throw such a work as that into the fire ?" " Hush! hush ! monseigneur," said Lully, " I knew what I was about ; I've another copy."

In the year 1672, by discreditable intrigues, Lully obtained the exclusive privilege, already accorded to others,* of opening in Paris, under the title of Royal Academy of Music, a theatre for the performance of opera ; and the fifteen years following this, down to the year of his death, in 1687, are those during which he established his claims to a place in the list of eminent musicians. Odious as was the personal character of Lully, it is impossible to deny him the possession of some very signal and great qualities. His industry was prodigious ; his perseverance indomitable ; his management of time, and his power of doing business would have done credit to a Minister of State. He had to form, and eventually succeeded in forming, his whole staff—actors, singers, orchestral performers, dancers, scene-painters, dressers, mechanicians, and I know not whom besides. He seems to have possessed in perfection the first of all powers for a public character—that of turning to account the talents of inferior men. He employed such even in the composition of his operas, restricting the exercise of his own talent to things that he knew no one could do for him. Powers like these, undisturbed in their exercise by scruples of any kind, raised Lully to a high pitch of worldly prosperity, and earned for him a very lasting reputation. Though his career was a short one, he not only realized a great fortune, but produced a number of works whose term of popularity has been longer than that of any others of the same kind that have yet

* Among them Cambert, who died in England shortly after, ruined and broken-hearted.

been given to the world. The oldest operas of which it can, in any sense, be said that they still " keep the stage" are the "Alceste" and "Orfeo" of Glück, first produced in 1761–4—just a century ago. Several of Lully's operas retained their hold on public favour as long as, and one of them even longer than, this ; his "Theseus" produced in 1665, lived till 1768—*i.e.*, for a hundred and three years.

Lully wrote in all nineteen operas. The favour with which the majority of these were received was no doubt partly due to the novelty of opera itself, to the skill of the performers—for histrionic skill is no new accomplishment in France—to the splendour of the dresses and decorations, to Court favour and fashion, and to the interest of the subjects of the libretti and the tact with which they were treated. In the seventeenth century the dramatic poet had but one difficulty in his choice of subject—*l'embarras de richesses*. The world of history, of fable and of fiction, classical and mediæval, was all before him, where to choose. The stories and adventures of Alcestis, Theseus, Proserpine, Perseus, Amadis, Armida, Acis and Galatea—beautiful always and then new—were some of the canvases whereon Quinault was to draw his outlines, and which Lully was to make glow with colour. But the skill neither of the poet nor of the theatrical machinist has ever alone made an operatic success ; and such success as is due altogether to style of performance dies of course with the performer. Some of Lully's operas, I repeat, kept the stage for a century ; and this unparalleled longevity must be attributed in a great measure to the music, which, however wanting in charm much of it might prove to us, had once the merit of novelty, is often beautiful in itself, and, so far as I have been able to study it, is eminently dramatic— *i.e.*, appropriate to the characters whose means of expresion it is, and to the situations in which they are thrown. Satisfactory proof of this could only be obtained by what we are none of us ever likely to witness—a theatrical performance of one of Lully's operas. But something may be made of extracts, and I will now ask you to listen to two.

The first of these is a Recitative and Air from the opera "Perseus." It falls to the share of no less portentous a personage than Medusa, and is in the opera assigned to a tenor voice. This falsification of sex is, of itself, an exceedingly ingenious contrivance. A tenor, I need not say, is and has the effect of a high voice under ordinary circumstances; but a tenor voice, issuing from a mask—a head still beautiful, though now so terrible as to turn beholders into stone—surmounting a female figure, would come upon the ear, not with its accustomed effect, but with an effect of preternatural, and to the ordinary hearer, unaccountable depth. Apart from these accessories and the scene, Lully's intention will, I think, be better realized by a contralto voice. I have therefore ventured to transpose this song from F into C.

In the first, or declamatory, portion, the expression of the very fine words, has no doubt, been the principal consideration with the composer. He has, however, not forgotten, in an over-attention to their sense, accent and quantity, that he had to express them through music; nor that, in setting them, he was subject to the conditions of musical art. The train of modulation, though varied and spontaneous, is thoroughly musician-like. The air, though stately, as suits the personage to whom it is assigned, is flowing and becoming to the voice. The accompaniment, to the recitative more especially (I have made not an "arrangement" but a literal transcription of the score), is most masterly, and shows that Lully was quite aware, among other things, how much the effect of a voice part may be increased by keeping the instrumental parts clear of it.

A song of a very different character, from the opera "Roland," will I think give you as high a notion of Lully as a composer of bright and clear melody as you may derive from the first song in respect to his energetic expression.

J'AI PERDU LA BEAUTÉ.

From the Opera "*Perseus.*"　　　　　　　　　　　J. B. Lully.

las fut ja-lou-se de mes ap - pas, Et me ren-dit af-

freuse au-tant que j'é-tois bel - le; Mais l'ex-cès é-ton-

nant de la dif-for-mi - té, Dont me pu-nit sa cru-au-

té, Fe-ra con-noître en dé-pit d'elle, Quel fut l'ex-cès de ma beau-

H

té; Je ne puis trop mon - trer sa ven - gean - ce cru -

el - le; Ma teste est fiere en - cor d'avoir pour or - ne - ment Des ser -

pents dont le sif - fie - ment Ex - ci - te une fray-eur mor - tel - le.

Andante marcato. (♩ = 96.)

Je por - te l'é - pou-

p

vante et la mort en tous lieux; Tout se change en ro - cher à

H 2

mon as - pect hor - ri - ble; Je ri - ble; Les traits que Ju - pi-

ter lan - ce du haut des cieux, N'ont rien de si ter-

ri - ble qu'un re - gard de mes yeux.

Les plus grands

Dieux du ciel, de la terre, et de l' onde, Du

soin de se ven - ger se re - po - sent sur moi; Les plus grands

1st

moi; Si je perds la dou - ceur d'ê - tre l'a - mour du

mond - e, J'ai le plai-sir nou - veau d'en de - ve - nir l'ef-

froi; Si je froi.

SONG.—ROLAND, COUREZ AUX ARMES.

From the Opera "*Roland.*" 1685.   J. B. LULLY.

pas, L'a - mour de ses   di - vins ap - pas,   Fait vi - vre au de-

là du tré - pas   Ro - land,   cou - rez   aux ar - mes, aux

ar - mes,   cou - rez   aux ar - mes, Que la

gloi - re a   de charm - es,   Que la   gloi - re a   de   charm - es.

As in other countries, side by side with but overshadowed by vocal, instrumental music made some progress in France during the seventeenth century; Mersenne makes mention of a good many instrumental writers and performers living in his time, the first half of it. But, as I have said before, they are, for the most part, to us mere names. Considerable interest in one of these has however been created or revived in our own time; and to it I must now call your attention.

Like the name Bach, the name Couperin represents an illustrious musical family, as well as an illustrious musician, the biographies of no less than ten members of which—two of them women—have been thought worthy of record. For the moment I shall only speak of François Couperin, one of the second generation known musically, and surnamed " Le Grand" in consequence of his superiority, as a performer on the organ and harpsichord, to all contemporary Frenchmen. This of itself would argue relative rather than absolute merit; for instrumental performance was no doubt at a low ebb in France at the beginning of the last century ; but as Couperin lived at the same time as Louis Marchand, a performer who, however unworthily, was once induced to enter lists with the great J. S. Bach, and as Couperin was thought superior to Marchand, there can be little doubt that the former was a great performer, none whatever that he was an ingenious, tasteful, and effective writer for his instrument. I will only preface the introduction of a specimen of his composition by saying that Le Grand Couperin was born at Paris in 1678, and died in 1733, and that he held the offices of organist in the Church of St. Gervais and the Chapel Royal, and of clavecinist to the King. The majority of Couperin's compositions are distinguished by titles indicative of some idea, person, or condition of mind which may have suggested them. That which you will now hear is entitled " La Voluptueuse."

LA VOLUPTUEUSE.

François Couperin.

But the greatest musical name of the first half of the last century (the end of the third period) in France, is that of Rameau, whose long and interesting career deserves more time and attention than we shall now have to give to it. He was born at Dijon in 1683, visited Italy early in life, and afterwards became a pupil of Marchand. Unsuccessful in obtaining a position in Paris, he accepted the office of organist to the cathedral of Clermont, in Auvergne. Rameau's residence in this remote and quiet city proved singularly favourable to the prosecution of certain researches in which he had long been engaged; and these resulted in the completion, after four years' labour, of a treatise on the science of Harmony. Proverbially " Paris is France ;" and to bringing his discoveries before the world, a residence in the capital became or seemed to Rameau an indispensable preliminary. There was an obstacle to this, however, in the agreement which he had made with the Chapter of Clermont to hold his office for a term of years, which agreement the Chapter, proud of their organist, altogether refused to terminate prematurely. Whereupon the too competent subordinate hit on an expedient more creditable to his cunning than his professional pride, and took to playing so abominably that the Bishop and his clergy were only too glad to come to any arrangement that would relieve their ears from the torture to which Rameau daily subjected them. Unwilling, however, that the unfavourable impression produced by his temporary musical aberrations should be permanent, the recusant organist is said to have poured forth such a rich and varied stream of harmony on the congregation at his farewell performance, that his late masters would willingly have rescinded his order of release. But it was too late.

Rameau arrived in Paris in 1721, and in the following year brought forth his " Traité d'Harmonie." " This work," says M. Fétis, " was at first not at all understood ;" but the critiques upon it, though unfavourable, were so far advantageous to

Rameau that they drew public attention upon him. Some pieces of vocal and instrumental chamber music which he published about the same time increased his notoriety ; and he soon found office as an organist, and large occupation as a teacher. Desirous of distinction in every branch of his calling, he connected himself with Piron, the dramatist, and by way of preparing himself for greater undertakings, wrote much incidental music—choruses, dances, &c., for Piron's plays. In 1726 he published his " Nouveau Système de Musique Théorique," and in 1732 his " Dissertation sur les différentes Méthodes d'Accompagnement pour le Clavecin et pour l'Orgue." In this same year, having arrived at the age of forty-nine, he succeeded in making his *début* as an opera composer. His first work, " Hippolyte et Aricie," was coldly received. Nor is this in the least surprising. For half a century past the music of Lully had exclusively occupied the Parisian ear and, as a consequence, formed the Parisian taste ; and any deviation from the Lullian style was regarded as the rankest and most unjustifiable musical heresy. The boldness and originality of Rameau were obstacles to his success—at first. Combinations which, so soon as the public ear had become habituated to them, were called vigorous, expressive, and original, were, on their first performance, denounced as cacophonous, unmeaning, and extravagant ; and their author was accused of indulging his own perverse passion for " harmonic experiments " at the expense of his Public's organs of hearing.* As a matter of course—for no musical inventor has escaped this—his music was pronounced altogether

---

* The following is one of many contemporary epigrams to the same effect :—

> Si le difficile est le beau,
> C'est un grand homme que Rameau ;
> Mais si le beau, par aventure,
> N'était que la simple nature,
> Quel petit homme que Rameau !

" Le beau " in Art is surely not identical with " la simple nature."

deficient in melody, which is often tantamount to saying that it does not abound with familiar and commonplace passages. The music of Rameau however did succeed eventually in making its way to the hearts of his countrymen, and during the remaining thirty years of his life (he died in 1764, at the age of eighty-one), he continued in undisturbed possession of the high place he had so slowly and painfully won.

The theoretical writings of Rameau have been translated into many languages, and his theories have been accepted or rejected—certainly, studied—wherever music is regarded as a matter worthy of serious consideration. Perhaps the rank assigned to him as a discoverer, by his countrymen, is rather higher than foreigners may be disposed to think him entitled to. His clearness of view and power of statement it would be difficult to overrate; and, at the lowest, Rameau is entitled to the credit of having been the first writer who ever attempted to systematize, account for, and reconcile a number of facts which, before his time, were held to be unconnected, inconsistent, and irreconcilable with one another. His vocal music, like that of Lully, has never made any success—indeed, it has rarely travelled—out of France; but some of what he no doubt regarded as the least important of his works, his compositions for the clavecin, have found very general acceptance and favour. Examples of these are not unfrequently met with in collections of pianoforte music; but I know not whither to refer you for specimens of his vocal compositions. The following Quartet will probably be new to most of you. It is from his opera "Les Indes Galantes," produced in 1735, and therefore one of his earliest essays in dramatic music. It presents many instances of those bold—or harsh—combinations for which Rameau has been both praised and blamed (note especially that in the last bar but four); but the composition has at least the merit of being vigorous and well-sustained.

QUARTET.—TENDRE AMOUR.

From "*Les Indes Galantes.*"   J. B. Rameau.

mais. Tendre A - mour. Que pour nous ta

mais. Tendre A - mour.

mais. Que pour nous ta chai - ne dure à ja-

mais. . . . . Que pour nous ta chai - ne

fz *p*

chai - ne dure à ja - mais, à ja - mais, à ja-

Que ta chai - ne dure à ja-

mais, à ja - mais, à ja-

dure à ja - mais, à ja - mais, à ja-

cres.

mais. Que pour nous ta chai - ne dure à ja - mais.

mais. Que pour nous ta chai - ne dure à ja - mais. Tendre A-

mais. Tendre A - mour, que ta

mais. Que ta

Tendre A-mour, tendre A-mour, tendre A - mour, que ta

mour, que ta chai - ne du - re à ja - mais, que ta

chai

chai

chai - ne dure à ja - mais, à ja - mais, que pour nous ta

chai - ne dure à ja - mais, à ja - mais, que pour

- ne dure à ja - mais, à ja - mais,

- ne dure à ja - mais, à ja - mais, que pour nous ta

chai - ne dure à ja - mais, ... à ja - mais, .

nous, que pour nous ta chai - ne dure à ja - mais, .

que pour nous ta chai - ne dure à ja - mais, .

chai - ne dure à ja - mais, ...

Of the numerous assailants whom the theoretical writings, the music, and the somewhat acrid temper and angularity of Rameau raised up against him, not the least formidable was J. J. Rousseau. For anything like general considerations of the character and writings of Rousseau this, of course, is not the time; but music occupies so large a space in his writings, and so greatly influenced his life, that it is impossible to dismiss even this very imperfect outline of French musical history in the third period without some notice of both.

Rousseau would seem to have been gifted with a fine musical organization, and under favourable circumstances he might have been made a musician. The time—and it was a good deal—which he devoted to music was about equally divided between sneering at everything which, for the last four hundred years, musicians and the mass of mankind have agreed to call music, and striving to make a reputation as a practitioner of this very art. His writings abound in disparaging contrasts between modern music and the music of the ancients—whatever that expression may mean—and in abuse (I can call it little else) of every artifice which gives interest to modern musical practice. His letter "Sur la Musique Françoise" is the best-known and the most accessible of these writings, all of which however will reward perusal; for Rousseau, I need not say, is always readable, whether he treats on a subject of which his knowledge is profound or his ignorance absolute. The apparent object of this letter is to prove that the French language is little fitted for poetical, and quite unfitted for musical, expression ; and he inaugurates the demonstration of this thesis by this remark :—" I do not hesitate to address myself on this subject to poets ; but as for musicians, no one would think of consulting them on any matter requiring the exercise of reason."

His real object in the letter would seem however to have been to glorify melody at the expense. of harmony, and to show that the chief obstacles to the perfection of modern music consisted in everything in relation to it worthy of the name of science. "The only effect," says he, "which can result from the aggregation of a number of melodies individually good is that they destroy one another, for it is impossible for the ear to take in at the same instant several melodies." Here we have a not uncommon example of generalization from a particular instance. That Rousseau's ear could not take in more than one melody at a time was likely enough ; that hundreds of ears *can* do so is a matter of daily experience. Again, he says of the orchestra,—" to make the violins play this passage, the flutes that, and the bassoons the other, each having its own particular design, and to call this chaos music, is to insult alike the ears and the judgments of an auditory." But the following is still more curious, not merely for the sentiment but likewise for the illustration :—" As for fugues, double fugues, fugues by inversion, augmentation or diminution—as for ground basses and other preposterous difficulties, that neither the ear can endure nor the reason justify—they are evidently relics of barbarism and bad taste which remain, like the portals of our Gothic churches, to the shame of those who have had the patience to build them."

With audacious inconsistency, the author of this and much more to the same effect produced several operas—the music as well as the words professedly his own;—not monophonous operas " after the manner of the ancients;" not revivals of that pure and beautiful Greek music which sweetly and submissively and subordinately contented itself with lending an additional grace to poetry; but unequivocal operas in the modern sense of the word, with duets, the parts of which were neither in unison nor in octaves, unless by accident, with concerted pieces still more widely divergent from classical usage,—nay, even an overture :— all these accompanied, not by the pipe of Pan, the lyre of Mercury, the salpinx, the syrinx, the cithara, the chelys, the psalterion, or the tibia utricularis, but by those Gothic abominations, the violin, the viola, the violoncello, and the violone— the self-same implements by the use of which Lully and Rameau, Scarlatti and Pergolesi, Handel and Bach, had been debasing the public taste for half a century before.

Rousseau's attacks on Rameau were not unprovoked. The former began his musical career by that commonest and easiest of all musical transactions—the invention of a new system of musicography. Unable, as indeed he remained to the end of his days, to master the alphabet of modern music—the only alphabet which has ever had the slightest pretension to the epithet " universal"—he set to work to devise another. This however the world obstinately refused to adopt, notwithstanding his eloquent *plaidoiries* against all existing alphabets, and in favour of his own. It was not exactly the old story of the

fox that had lost his tail, but rather of a single and exceptional
"tailless variety" of fox who had never known the advantage of
that comely and convenient appendage. This scheme proving
abortive, he turned his hand, as I have said, to opera. His
first attempt was entitled "Les Muses Galantes," which was
actually performed in Paris, at the house of the Fermier Général,
Popelinière. Rameau, who was domestic musician-in-chief to
this establishment, took part, as a matter of course, in the
rehearsals and performance of this opera; and declared, very
ineloquently no doubt, but very decisively, that it was the work
of two hands, the one an artist, the other an utter ignoramus.
Five minutes' association at a rehearsal must have convinced a
musician like Rameau that the better parts of "Les Muses
Galantes" could not be the work of Rousseau; and Rameau, as
it was not in the least likely that he should, did not conceal his
opinion. Rousseau never forgave him.

Some years of subsequent undirected and fitful application did
however give Rousseau some knowledge of the science about
which he had already written so much and so disparagingly.
"Docendo disces" might have been his motto in respect to the
theory of music. In the art he made little improvement; never,
it is believed, having attained to anything beyond the slowest
appreciation of the relations between notes and the musical
effects represented by their infinitely various combinations and
successions. The cause of this is simple enough. Rousseau
had never received any systematic training in music at the only
time such training can be effectual. This is greatly to be
regretted. His musical organization was undoubtedly fine; and
had he fallen early enough into good hands, he would no doubt
have done something both beautiful and original. His compositions, or rather concoctions, which have seen the light, timid
and laboured as they are, give evidence of far better intentions
than their author was at all able to carry into effect. He would
seem to have been the first composer who added instrumental

accompaniment to spoken dialogue—a use of the orchestra which, though seemingly calculated to impair the reality of dramatic performance, is unquestionably very effective; serving to point and intensify action, while adding to it the charm of another art.

Rousseau made several attempts, besides that I have already mentioned, at dramatic music. One of these, and one only, attained anything like success, " Le Devin au Village," which, first performed in 1752, kept its place on the French stage for sixty years. Rousseau's claim to the authorship of the music has been again and again contested, but it is now generally agreed that the essential portions of the work were his, though in some of the details he must have received help. The music of his melodrama " Pygmalion" has been attributed to a musician named Coignet, but no claimant has been set up for that of the " Devin au Village." The posthumous collection of vocal music which he entitled " Les Consolations des Misères de ma Vie" is undisputedly his work. It consists wholly of airs of the most simple construction and, generally, plaintive character. In going over them some years since I marked those I thought worthy of especial note. The two best of these few you shall now hear. The first, " Je l'ai planté," is a very favourable specimen of Rousseau's manner—a simple and unpretending, but surely very touching melody. The slight variation at the end of the last stanza is the composer's own.

The second song is fairly entitled to such admiration as is due to every contest with difficulty, even though it be self-imposed. The melody consists of only thr e notes. Why a song should be constructed after the pattern of an orchestral drum-part might have puzzled even its eloquent author to explain. The result, however, is quaint and pleasing. The first phrase will remind you of the well-known French air, " Au Clair de la Lune." Whether of the two airs was composed first I am unable to say.

AIR.—JE L'AI PLANTÉ.

J. J. ROUSSEAU.

Con tenerezza.

1st ver. Je l'ai plan - té, je l'ai vu nai - tre Ce beau ro-
2nd ver. Jo-yeux oi - seaux, troupe a - mou - reu - se, Ah! par pi-
3rd ver. Pour les tré - sors du nou - veau Mon - de Il fuit l'a

sier où les oi - seaux Vien-nent chan - ter, sous ma fe-
tié, ne chan - tez pas; L'a-mant qui me ren - dit heu-
mour, bra - ve la mort, He - las! pour - quoi cher-cher sur

nê - tre, Per - chés sur ses jeu - nes ra - meaux.
reu - se Est par - ti pour d'au-tres cli - mats.
l'on - de Le bon - heur qu'il trou-vait au port!

4th ver. Vous pas - sa - gè - res hi - ron - del - les, Qui re - ve-

nez cha - que prin - temps, Oiseaux sen - si - bles et fi-

dè - les, Ra - me - nez le moi tous les ans.

AIR DE TROIS NOTES.—QUE LE JOUR ME DURE.

J. J. ROUSSEAU.

Allegretto.

Que le jour me du - re, Pas - sé loin de toi,
He - las! si je pas - se Un jour sans te voir,
Le cœur me pal - pi - te, Quand j'en-tens ta voix,

Tou - te la na - tu - re N'est plus rien pour moi:
Je cher-che ta tra - ce Dans mon dés - es - poir:
Tout mon sang s'a - gi - te Dès que je te vois:

Le plus verd boc - ca - ge, Quand tu n'y viens pas,
Quand je l'ai per - due, Je res - te a pleu - rer,
Ou - vre tu ta bou - che, Les cieux vont s'ou - vrir,

N'est qu'un lieu sau - va - ge, Pour moi sans ap - pas.
Mon âme é - per - du - e Est près d'es - pi - rer.
Si ta main me tou - che, Je me sens fre - mir.

LECTURE IV.

GERMANY.

HEINRICH SCHÜTZ—CANTATA, "THE FINDING OF THE SAVIOUR"—THE THIRTY YEARS' WAR—ORGANISTS AND ORGANS—THE CLAVICHORD—GEORGE MUFFAT—"NOVA CYCLOPEIAS HARMONICA"—REINHARD KEISER—AIR, "O ABBA, FATHER"—HASSE AND GRAUN—J. SEBASTIAN BACH—RECITATIVE AND AIR FROM HIS PASSIONS-MUSIK—C. E. EMMANUEL BACH—FANTASIA.

LECTURE IV.

GERMANY.

GERMANY contributes some great names to the history of the third period: though the third is not the great period of German musical history. Handel's long expatriation almost warrants our excluding him from the list of German musical worthies. The most important works of Glück belong rather to the beginning of the fourth than to the end of the third period. Moreover they owe much to foreign inspiration; for the two "Iphigenies" and "Armide" are, all three, French operas—the earliest only begun in 1774, when the composer was sixty years of age. The name of John Sebastian Bach is truly a great one: but what single name, however great, can be put in comparison with those which make up the glorious company that succeeded him—Haydn, Mozart, Beethoven, Schubert, Spohr, Weber, Schumann and Mendelssohn?

I have on a former occasion shown how largely indebted is the Italian School to the Belgian, and how much of its development, if not of its inspiration, the former owes to Josquin Des-près, Goudimel and others who, in the first half of the sixteenth century, introduced the artifices of part-writing to the South of Europe;—for these men were the teachers of Palestrina and others, through whom their traditions, widened, deepened and beautified exceedingly, have been passed on by careful and reverential hands almost to our own time; since, so late as 1714, Tommaso Bai made an addition, which has proved permanent, to the music of the Holy Week at Rome, and Janacconi, musically the last of the Romans, lived till the beginning of the present century (1816).

The obligations of the Italians to their Northern teachers have been amply acknowledged; and, it should be added, returned with interest. To the Italians recent German music owes much, directly and indirectly. We shall see by-and-by, for example, what the School of Naples did for the Anglo-German composer, Handel. But for the moment let us confine our attention to a more distant example in every sense, one to whom the Germans themselves have given the honourable and affectionate title of "the Father of German music." This patriarch of harmony, Heinrich Schütz, whose name may now be heard by many of you for the first time, was born at Koesteritz in the Voigtland, in 1585. His beautiful voice drew attention to him as a boy, and, by a rare deviation from the ordinary course of things, was a means of, not an impediment to, his receiving a good general education. He distinguished himself very greatly at the University of Marburg, especially in the study of jurisprudence, cultivating his talent for music meanwhile with great zeal, and such success as to attract the notice of the Margrave Maurice, who sent him, at his own charge, to Venice, to study under Giovanni Gabrieli, then at the very height of his celebrity as a composer and teacher, but unfortunately nearly at the end of his career. The intimate relations which existed at this time between Venice and the great commercial cities of Germany rendered this a very natural proceeding. Venetian art was no less familiar, in the sixteenth century, to the citizens of Dresden or Nuremburg, than Venetian commerce. Gabrieli's relations with the North of Europe were close and extensive. He was again and again tempted to take up his residence in this or that German Court or Capital, but the attraction of his native city was too strong for him. He never quitted Venice. Some notion of the estimation in which he was held by his contemporaries may be got from the following passage, written many years afterwards by Schütz himself :—" I served my first years of apprenticeship in music under the great Gabrieli : Ye Immortal Gods, what a man was that ! If the ancients, so rich in expression, had been acquainted with his powers they would have set him above the Amphions : and if "—here Schütz touches, or oversteps, the confines of the sublime—" and if the Muses had been inclined to enter the marriage state, Melpomene would have desired no other husband than he, so great was he in his art."

Schütz remained at Venice three years, at the end of which (in 1612) Gabrieli died. He then returned to Germany, whence, after sixteen years of residence, he was driven, by the misery and confusion consequent on the Thirty Years' War, then in its tenth year. He returned in 1628 to Venice, not merely as a place endeared to him by a thousand pleasant reminiscences, the sight of which—after a sixteen years' episode, including much domestic affliction, as well as an unavoidable participation in public calamity—would in some sense renew to him the time of his youth, but for a special reason which he himself has taken the trouble to record. " I returned," he says, " to Venice, to make myself acquainted with the *new kind of music* which had been developed there since I last left it." This expression, " new kind of music," refers of course to the compositions of Monteverde and his imitators, of which I have already so often spoken, and affords in itself a valuable piece of unconscious and incidental evidence of the importance attached to it by Monteverde's contemporaries.

After a residence of six years in Venice and other Italian cities, Schütz returned to Germany, to find less opportunity than ever for the exercise of his peaceful art. He passed on to Copenhagen, where, meeting with a very enthusiastic reception, he remained four years, returning for a short time to Germany, then back again to Denmark, and finally to his native country, never again to leave it. The last years of his life were passed

K

in Dresden, where he died, in the year 1672, at the good old age of eighty-seven, in the fullest enjoyment of

> that which should accompany old age,
> As honour, love, obedience, troops of friends.

The career of Henry Schütz resembles in many respects that of his great countryman, Handel, and in none more than its termination. Schütz, like Handel, gave up his last years to the composition of sacred music, doubtless with the same feeling as that which actuated Handel; because, as the latter is recorded to have said, the composition of sacred music especially became a musician descending in the scale of years. In one important particular these two distinguished men differ. Handel, early in life, threw off all connexion with his native country. With insignificant exceptions, his operas were all Italian, his oratorios all English. Schütz, with all his wanderings, never lost his nationality. He is essentially a German— a composer and a man of whom his countrymen have just cause to be proud. With the exception of a book of Madrigals published in 1511, during his first residence in Venice, and a few Latin motets, all his numerous compositions were inspired by German texts. These are for the most part sacred works. He is distinguished, however, as the composer of the first German opera—a translation by Opitz of Rinuccini's "Daphne." This work, the composition of which is an epoch in the history of music, was produced in 1627.

Copies of the printed works of Schütz have now become exceedingly rare; nor do we often find even fragments of them among the selections and collections of Ancient Classical Music, so many of which have of late years issued from the German press. Three of his arrangements of ancient chorales are given in Winterfield's " Evangelische Kirchengesang ;" but several much more characteristic specimens of his manner may be found in a very recent and more accessible work, Reissmann's " Allgemeine

Geschichte der Musik." Some of these are extracted from a composition in MS., in the public library at Dresden, " The Passion," four settings of which, after the accounts of the four Evangelists, Schütz made in his eighty-first year. In these the several acts of that tremendous drama are presented in music of extraordinary energy, variety, and appropriateness. There is possibly some even earlier work of the kind with which I am unacquainted ; but, so far as my own reading extends, Schütz's " Passion according to St. Matthew" is the type not only of the more elaborate treatments of Bach and Handel (for two early works of this kind by Handel have recently been made known), but of that class of oratorio of which Mendelssohn's " St. Paul" is so fine an example, and which the unfinished " Christus" by the same master promised at least to equal.

A performance of these choral fragments, not by a chorus but by a quartet, and detached, as they must be, from their context, would convey bnt a faint idea of their effect in the work to which they belong, especially having regard to its early date. Another work which I have been fortunate enough to find will give you, I think, a better idea of the genius and culture of this composer. It is a sort of little oratorio or cantata—a musical illustration of that touching scene of which so fine and original a pictorial illustration has recently been given by Mr. Holman Hunt—the finding of the Saviour in the Temple. It is, fortunately for our present purposes, not long, and you shall hear it entire. It consists of an introduction for stringed instruments, a duet for Contralto and Bass, and a solo for a Soprano. In the introduction, which is in five real parts, the second subject of the duet which follows it is incidentally treated, quite in the manner of a modern overture. For the sake of contrast and keeping, this duet is accompanied by a bass and clavichord only, but in the concluding solo the stringed instruments are re-introduced, doubtless with a view of giving it greater dignity, and concluding the work with more striking effect.

SINFONIA.

HEINRICH SCHÜTZ.
(1650.)

DUETTO.

L'istesso tempo.

MARY. My Son, my Son, wherefore hast thou thus

JOSEPH.

dealt with us? My

My Son, my Son, wherefore hast thou thus dealt with

Son, my Son, my Son, wherefore hast thou thus dealt . . . .

us? My Son, my Son, my Son, wherefore hast thou thus

. . . with us? Wherefore hast thou thus dealt with

dealt with us? Wherefore hast thou thus dealt . . . . . with

us? Be - hold Thy fa - ther and I,

us? Be hold Thy mo-ther and

Thy fa - ther and I, Thy fa - ther and

I Thy mo - ther and I, Thy mo - ther and

I, we have sought thee sor - - - - row - ing, sor-

I, we have sought thee sor - row-

- - row - ing, Thy fa - ther and I,

ing, sought sor - row - ing, Thy mo-ther and

SOLO.

It is one of the most curious facts connected with the history of music that, at the close of the Thirty Years' War, Germany was found to be provided, and not at all insufficiently, with a body of very learned contrapuntists and skilful organists; proving, of course, that an art and science which one would picture to oneself as the very incarnation of political quiescence, had found diligent practitioners and students during the most sanguinary and protracted struggle that had ever cursed a great and civilized nation. Such, however, was the case. The Thirty Years' War extended from 1618 to 1648. During those years, Hans and Christopher Bach, Schütz, Scheidt, Scheidemann, and many others, cultivated, practised, and must have taught their art; since they were almost immediately succeeded by J. Amboise Bach, Kerl, Froberger, Theile, and Zackau, who, in his turn, became nothing less than the teacher of Handel.

Again, skilful organists imply of necessity organs of a certain scale, completeness, and finish. Of all musical performers the organist is most at the mercy of his instrument, perfection in the complex mechanism of which is simply indispensable to effective performance. Before the middle of the seventeenth century the organ must have attained to something very like perfection in Germany. Indeed, before the expiration of the preceding century (the sixteenth) almost every essential peculiarity of the modern organ was invented,—registers, stopped pipes, reed and various imitative stops, and pipes of small scale. So also the key-board had been extended to four octaves (nearly its present compass), and the pedal-board (an invention of the fifteenth century) had been universally adopted. It would be reasonable to suppose that during the Thirty Years' War more organs were destroyed than built; yet it is certain that it was in the course of the seventeenth century that Germany became, above all others, the land of great organs and great organists.

Nor were the domestic keyed instruments less cultivated in Germany, at the epoch of which I am speaking, than those whose use was limited to Divine Worship. Several of the organists whom I have named were able to touch with equal skill, and hardly less science, the clavicytherium, the clavichord, and the spinet. Others devoted themselves to this class of instrument exclusively. Of these one of the most distinguished was George Muffat, who early in life found his way to Paris, and received instruction from Lully. He began his professional career as organist of the Cathedral of Strasburg, from which city, being driven out by one of the "Crusades" of Louis XIV., he proceeded to Vienna, and subsequently to Rome, where he resided for several years. In 1690 he returned to Germany, and became organist and chapel-master, first to the Archbishop of Salzburg, and then to the Bishop of Passau. The year of his death, as of his birth, is unknown. These particulars, with some others, are recorded in a preface to one of his works (a collection of instrumental concerted pieces), written in four languages, Latin, Italian, French, and German. Muffat was evidently desirous of securing to himself a large public.

In one of his works, entitled "Apparatus Musico-organisticus," published at Augsburg in 1695, is a piece called "Nova Cyclopeias Harmonica," a title which may have suggested that of the more recent "Harmonious Blacksmith." It consists of an Air in two sections, followed by another headed "Ad Malleorum Ictus Allusio," to which are added seven variations. This melody is singularly constructed ; it begins with a sequence formed by the repetition of the initiatory phrase, which is in C, first in A minor, then in F major. The variations are devoid of those extended arpeggios which afterwards became so common ; but they are crowded, to excess, with shakes, trills, and mordenti ; indeed there is hardly a place in them which would bear a shake which is left without one.

There is a piece in Dr. Rimbault's History of the Pianoforte by *Theophilus* Muffat, which contains the germ of Handel's March in "Judas Maccabeus." This composer was the son of George Muffat, whose "Nova Cyclopeias Harmonica" you will now hear.

TOCCATA.

GEORG MUFFAT.

Ad malleorum ictus allusio.

sæpius repetita valebunt.

The history of German opera is commonly considered to begin with the works of Reinhard Keiser, though, as we have seen, he had a predecessor in Heinrich Schütz. Schütz, however, seems to have had no imitators or immediate successors.

Reinhard Keiser was born at a village near Leipzig in 1673. His musical education, begun by his father, was completed in the celebrated School of St. Thomas, at Leipzig. The particular bent of his genius showed itself early; he produced his first work, a sort of pastoral, at the age of nineteen, and his second, an opera, " Basileus," two years afterwards.

He entered on his career at an auspicious moment, when the German operatic stage, recently altogether dependent on Italian or French sources, or at least on works of foreign model, was beginning to tolerate and encourage native efforts. Attracted by reports of the flourishing condition of the theatre at Hamburg, Keiser succeeded in getting his opera played, and eventually in making himself a position, in that city. This he held for forty years, in the course of which, besides much other music, he composed and produced, according to a contemporary biographer, as many as a hundred and sixteen operas.

Extravagant encomium is no novel characteristic of musical criticism. The somewhat wasteful expenditure of laudatory epithets which come daily under the notice of all of us —especially in respect to music of whose excellence no one entertains the smallest doubt, and musicians who have long been in every sense beyond the reach of praise or blame—would seem to be as old as music itself. To tell you, therefore, that Keiser's contemporaries and immediate successors spoke and wrote about him as the greatest genius the world had ever seen, would be to tell what has been said and written many times before about many other people. Contemporaries like Mattheson and Hasse, however, compel our attention ; and it would have been difficult for them to have spoken of Keiser—of his originality, fecundity, and science—more highly than they have done. When we learn too that Handel made the first use of his liberty, as a young man, to visit Hamburg during Keiser's reign,—that *he* was content to enter his orchestra in quite a subordinate capacity, evidently that he might have opportunities of studying his modes of operation as a composer and conductor,—we are obliged to believe that in Keiser we have to do with a man of altogether exceptional powers. Circumstantial evidence is the more valuable in this case on account of the extreme rarity of copies of Keiser's works. Few of his operas, to which he owes most of his fame, were ever printed in any complete form ; even the titles of a very large number of them are irrecoverably lost ; and of his other works copies are so rare as to be, for all practical purposes, non-existent. There are, however, in Winterfeld's " Evangelische Kirchengesang," a few extracts from one of his Sacred Works, " The Passion," a subject treated by almost every eminent composer of the third period.

One of these, an air for a bass voice, with an oboe *obbligato,* you shall hear.

SOLO.—O ABBA, FATHER!

From "*The Passion*," Luke xxii. 42.   REINHARD KEISER (1712).

O Ab - ba, Fa - ther! if Thou be

will - ing,   remove this cup,   this cup   from me.

Ne - ver - the - less not my   will, not my   will, but

Thine be done, Ne - ver - the - less not my will, not

my will but Thine be done.

I had not long been engaged in the preparation of these lectures before I found that I had undertaken to do more than I should have time for. I shall not trouble you with any regrets at having to dismiss briefly two men whose names figure in my syllabus—Hasse and Graun—men whose careers and whose fortunes present many points of resemblance, both of whom enjoyed, during their lives, at least as much public favour as they deserved, and one of whom, Graun, still maintains, in his native country, an amount of it that it is not easy to account for. The "Tod Jesu" and the "Te Deum" of Graun are still, I believe, often performed in Germany; but Hasse is to the world at large, Germany included, now a mere name, and is, I think, likely to remain such. Yet (so much harder is it to estimate contemporaries than predecessors) among the many compliments paid to this composer during his lifetime, Hasse actually received an invitation to visit this country—as the rival of Handel! His own estimate of himself was, however, lower and juster than that of his inviters; for his answer is said to have been—"Then Handel, I suppose, is dead."

But I do feel my limits as to time strongly, in having now to speak of John Sebastian Bach—of all musicians the most difficult to estimate fairly; whose reputation among the learned in music and the unlearned is so widely discrepant, that while, by many among the former, he is regarded as the most original, the most inventive, the most suggestive, and therefore the most interesting, of composers, on the majority of the latter he has never directly exercised any but the feeblest influence—if even that. I am of course not unaware that some few pieces from his hand—instrumental works especially—have had attention drawn to them of late by the "interpretation" (as the phrase is) of certain eminent performers. But much of the admiration which they have, under these circumstances, called forth, must surely be attributed to the marvellous skill of these performers, and to the sense of satisfaction which all

observers have in a successful contest with difficulty—a spec-
tacle in which even the Gods are said to take pleasure. With
the initiated, for the moment, I have no concern. But I presume
the most enthusiastic worshipper of Bach that lives will not
hesitate to admit—nay, he will rather glory in avowing—that,
as compared with Handel, Haydn, Mozart, Beethoven—to say
nothing of writers of another class—his idol is utterly unknown
to the world at large.

How is this? Who is to blame? These questions admit of
more than one answer.

The ultimate use and purpose of Fine Art are to instruct
and to inform. In these particulars of course it is not
singular or alone. But it differs from, and has perhaps an
advantage over, other humanizing agencies in the fact of its
effecting, or seeking to effect, its purposes, by means which *of
themselves* give pleasure. This pleasure will vary in its inten-
sity according to the susceptibility of those to whom it is to
be given; and this susceptibility, to whatever extent it may or
may not be natural, is capable of great increase by cultivation.
Now, it is notorious that the great mass of mankind do not put
their susceptibilities under any sort of culture, in any systematic way, for any length of time; nor, in other words, do they
accept Fine Art as a science, and study it, and deal with it,
accordingly. The consequence of this inevitably is that works
of art—poems, pictures, statues, and, more than all, pieces of
music—have been, and perhaps always will be, produced in
considerable numbers, which neither have had, nor ever can
have, the smallest direct influence on the world at large; for
there always have been, as again there always will be, many
artists—poets, painters, sculptors, or musicians—whose facility
or felicity of expression, whose method of putting things, or
whose power of statement, is so far inferior to their conception and intention—in a word, whose *style* is of itself so devoid
of charm—that their thought, however original or profound,

never has reached, never, it is to be feared, will reach, the great mass of readers, spectators, or auditors.

The question then is whether this great mass—the world at large, the uninitiated—are the more to blame for not appreciating such works of art, or the artists themselves for producing them. And the answer to this question is involved in that to another ;—is any sacrifice of self-respect entailed on an artist by the endeavour to extend the sphere of his direct influence as largely as possible ? or, to put it in another way, is pure and beautiful thought inconsistent with clear and beautiful expression ?

I think not. The history of music at least surely teaches us that the pure and the beautiful may and often do find a response in the common heart ; for, some of the most popular works in existence are also some in which there is the least evidence of sacrifice of self-respect on the part of their composers. Nay, I will say more ; the musical works which have taken the strongest hold on the musical public—which, remember, is not a mere national public, but a public of all nations—are those whose internal structure reveals to an observant eye and ear not merely the most copious inventiveness and the most delicate sense of beauty, but the profoundest science.

Think of the " Hallelujah Chorus" in Handel's " Messiah," of Mozart's overture to "·Zauberflöte,"—the list might be extended indefinitely. Where is the sacrifice of self-respect shown in the composition of these pieces ? where the evidence of writing down to the level of an ignorant public ? Where, indeed ? But the makers of these works possessed, one and all, that indispensable complement to the highest genius—never dissevered from it—good sense. And good sense taught them that to be heard they must speak plainly, to be understood they must speak clearly ; and that even diamonds and pearls, uncut and unpolished, if thrown at people's heads, will not find that grateful acceptance which a little exercise of the lapidary's skill, and a more courteous delivery, would have insured them.

Clearness of expression, so necessary in all the arts, is especially requisite in two of them—music and the drama. For these exist, for the world at large, not in space, but in time. A lyric or an epic poem, a building, a statue, or a picture, is a fact permanently open to our study and consideration. If we do not succeed in understanding it to-day, we may try to do so again to-morrow. But, to the mass of mankind, an unperformed piece of music, or an unacted play, is non-existent; and if it be not— I do not say perfectly understood, but—to some extent felt, on a first hearing, there is little likelihood of its ever being understood or felt at all. A musical hearer can no more stop the course of a musical performance, to any good purpose, than he can stop the course of time itself. A passage is not even complete for him till it has become a thing of the past.

It may be difficult at first to understand how a distinction between matter and manner, between thought and expression, can with propriety be made in reference to music. To the mass of mankind music *is* expression, and nothing else.

In one way, out of many, that will be easily understood. A musical composer may be laboriously incomprehensible and perversely unmeaning, by putting too much into his score,—by making one figure obscure another, or (technically) by piling part on part, passage on passage, till analysis becomes difficult, even for the eye, and impossible for the ear, and the result comes to resemble rather the incoherent cries of a mob than the clear utterances of a succession of thoughtful speakers.

Again, the musical composer, like the dramatic poet, but unlike other artists, acts on the public *in*directly—through the medium of others. And, if he would act efficiently on the former, he must in some degree consult the powers—nay, the tastes—of the latter. It must be admitted that no musical passage could be written, within the compass of a particular voice or instrument, which a skilful performer should not be able to execute. But the difference between the most skilful performer's execution of that which is becoming to his voice or instrument and that which is not, is like the difference between walking on a well-rolled pathway and floundering over a ploughed field.

To the charges of want of clearness in his own utterances, and absolute indifference to the convenience of those who were to be the interpreters of them, which they (and who can wonder at it?) have been often too ready to resent, J. S. Bach is, I think, often open. That these drawbacks on the enjoyment of his works, even among the learned, are to be accounted for in his manner of life—his entire freedom from competition, and the arrogance which a seemingly unapproachable excellence and an *entourage* of altogether inferior persons and things inevitably beget—is certain. But that, with all these drawbacks, the music of this master remains and must remain material whose height and depth will afford subject for the wonder and the love of the few who will ever be able to scale or to sound it, is as much so. The strongest sense of his merits is not unlikely to be connected with the strongest sense of his defects; and these latter, alas! are of a kind that, as they always have prevented, so, I think, they always will prevent, the former exercising their due and legitimate influence.

We must not, of course, part from this great master without some tribute of respect. This we will pay, not by trying to read one of his riddles or explaining away one of his paradoxes, but by showing that at times he could be clear as well as deep, and that careful and skilful performance may render one of not the least simple of his productions intelligible, even on a first hearing.

You shall hear two successive movements from one of the only two* of his great works that have yet been heard in England, " The Passion," according to St. Matthew.

---

* The other was, when this was written, the Credo from his Mass in B minor, performed under my direction at St. Martin's Hall in 1851.

RECITATIVE.—ALTHOUGH MINE EYES.

From the "*Passions-Musik.*"   J. S. BACH.

Al - though mine eyes with tears o'er- flow Be - cause . . . . . my Sa - viour leaves me now, My heart re - joic - es in His Tes - ta - ment, His Flesh and Blood, most pre - cious gift!

M

To me be - queathes He in my hand.

As He His own did love while here He

so - journ'd, Though now He reigns in Hea - ven, He

loves . . . them still un - to the end.

ARIA.—" JESUS, SAVIOUR."

J. S. Bach.

Andante con moto.

Je - sus, Sa - viour, I am Thine, Come and dwell, come .

. . . and dwell, come . . . . . and dwell my . . heart within,

Je - sus, Sa - viour, I am Thine, Come .. and dwell

... my heart within, Je - sus, Sa - viour, I am Thine ..

. . . . Come . . . and dwell my

. . heart with - in, Come . . . . . . and dwell my heart within.

Fine.

All things else I count but loss . . Glo-ry on - ly

in thy cross, Dear-er than the world be - side, Is the Sa - viour

. . . . who hath died.

All things else I count,

I count but loss, Glo - ry in Thy cross, Dear - er

than the world Is the Sa - viour who hath died.

D. C.

The name Bach, as I have already had occasion incidentally to notice, represents not only an individual but a race. The progeny of John Sebastian, like the ancestry, include many excellent and some very distinguished musicians. I have time to notice only one of these, Carl Philip Emmanuel Bach, whose life and works might furnish material for more than one long and interesting session. One, and that the main fact about him, may fortunately be stated in a few words; that he is, if any individual can be so called, the founder of the modern school of composition for, and performance on, the pianoforte. Not that the pianoforte was his instrument. He belongs to the harpsichord age; and his instrument was by no means the best, even of its kind. You will find a full and interesting account of him in Dr. Burney's " Present State of Music in Germany" (1775); and a part of it is devoted to his performance on the clavichord, an instrument which in the latter part of the last century must have been old-fashioned, but which still kept its favour. Dr. Burney says :

" After I had looked at these (some portraits), M. Bach was so obliging as to sit down to his Silbermann clavichord, and favourite instrument, upon which he played three or four of his choicest and most difficult compositions, with the delicacy, precision, and spirit for which he is so celebrated among his countrymen. In the pathetic and slow movements, whenever he had a long note to express, he absolutely contrived to produce, from his instrument, a cry of sorrow and complaint, such as can only be effected upon the clavichord, and perhaps by himself."

Of C. P. E. Bach we have something more enduring than the record of his skill as a performer—a large number of compositions in which a careful student will discern the germs, and a good deal more, of much of that which he finds so delightful in the later productions of Mozart and Beethoven. Emmanuel Bach was one of the first who threw his musical ideas into the "form" now universally adopted for the principal movement of a Sonata, Symphony, or other similar work. Perhaps he was the very first who did this effectively. The characteristic of this form, as I have elsewhere explained more fully, is the presentation of the most important themes, first in the scale or key of the dominant (to the original scale), and subsequently in that of the tonic; this repetition forming the second "period" or section of the movement, and being connected with the first by the "free fantasia" (*Ger.* Dürchführung), in which these themes are presented in every conceivable variety of aspect. Into this form not only did Emmanuel Bach, as I have just said, throw his ideas—of itself no easy matter now, and far more difficult a century ago, before Haydn had written or Mozart come into the world—but the ideas themselves exhibit an amount of inventiveness and refinement in which few writers have equalled, and none but the greatest surpassed, him.

A large number of Emmanuel Bach's works are still unpublished, but so much attention has of late been directed to those which are in any way accessible, that it is not unlikely we may eventually see all of them in print. Meanwhile, I will call your attention to the volume I now hold in my hand, which is a collection, edited by M. Fétis, of his pieces—so interesting, one and all, that I have had some difficulty in deciding which of them I should bring under your notice. I have selected, from a Sonata which consists of the usual number of movements, the third and last—a *Fantaisie*, full of bold modulation and sudden changes of time, introduced however with so much art, that they seem rather illustrations of, than digressions from, the principal theme. You will not fail to recognise many effects which will be familiar to you in the works of Beethoven, who was eighteen years of age when E. Bach died (at the age of eighty-two),—especially the very grand and unexpected transition near the close.

FANTAISIE.

C. P. E. Bach.

Larghetto sostenuto.

Fantaisie.

LECTURE V.

ENGLAND.

THE ENGLISH SCHOOL—ITS DURATION—EARLY ENGLISH
MUSIC—DUNSTABLE—EXPRESSION—HENRY LAWES—
DOWLAND AND FORD—SONGS, "WHILE I LISTEN TO
THY VOICE," AND "GO, YOUNG MAN"—ENGLISH INSTRU-
MENTAL MUSIC—NORTH'S "MEMOIRES"—JOHN JENKINS
—THREE-PART FANCY—THE INTERREGNUM—THE RE-
STORATION—PELHAM HUMPHREYS—PEPYS' "DIARY"
—ANTHEM, "HEAR, O HEAVENS!"—BLOW, WISE, AND
PURCELL—THE PERFECT CADENCE—MUSICAL IMITA-
TION—PURCELL—SONGS, "YOU TWICE TEN HUNDRED
DEITIES," "I ATTEMPT FROM LOVE'S SICKNESS TO FLY,"
"FULL FATHOM FIVE," AND "COME UNTO THESE
YELLOW SANDS."

LECTURE V.

ENGLAND.

WHATEVER claims—and they are very strong claims—we English may have to be called a musical people, it cannot be pretended that we have exercised much—some would say, any—influence on Continental music. That this is attributable, not to any inferiority, real or supposed, in our music, but altogether to our insular position, might be shown in many ways. It is sufficiently shown in a single fact. When Haydn first visited London (in 1791), he had never heard performed any one of the oratorios of Handel, who had then been dead more than forty years. Handel, I need hardly tell you, spent all his artistic life in England; and from this cause, although a German by birth, his works, the latest of them now more than a century old, and but few of these, have only recently attained anything that can be called popularity or circulation in his native country. They are still but very little known in any other part of Europe.

I have already, more than once, called your attention to the fact that three peoples—the Gallo-Belgians, the Italians, and the Germans—have taken the lead in musical Europe successively; the Gallo-Belgian school having been superseded by the Italian, and the Italian by the German, which, following a universal law, will doubtless be superseded in its turn by some other. The English school has a claim not only on *our* sympathy as Englishmen, but on the respect of every musical people as having had a career equal in extent or duration to that of all other schools added together.

The early records of these islands abound in evidence direct and indirect of the intense love and diligent culture of music among our forefathers, and of the high honour paid to the art and its professors, in the remotest times of which we have any credible account. Druid, bard, scald, and other such words, all having their different shades of meaning, but have all reference to musical practitioners of some kind or other,—some having been personages of the highest political or religious importance. The ancient languages of Great Britain are singularly rich in musical terms, and present names, more especially of musical instruments, some of which have come down, in slightly modified forms, to the present day. " Harp" is one of these ; " pipe" is another : and more interesting than any, as throwing light on the early history or origin of the instrument itself, is the word *fithele*—whence fiele, viel, viola, and at last violin, for almost every portion of which instrument a name of English origin exists—*e.g.* bridge, back, sound-post, bow.

The most recent writer on early English music, my friend Mr. William Chappell, has, in the introduction to his delightful volumes of " Popular Music of the Olden Time," presented a body of information on this subject which, in quantity, arrangement, and general interest, at once resumes and surpasses the results of any preceding labour of the same kind. I am glad to be able to refer those who are curious in the early lyrical and musical history of England to a work so readable and so thoroughly trustworthy as Mr. Chappell's.

Dismissing, as I must now do, this remote though interesting period of English musical history, it is certain that England gave birth, early in the fifteenth century, to a composer who has been more often alluded to, and always respectfully, by Continental musical historians and critics than any other native of these islands whatever. John Dunstable, who died in 1458, attained so great a reputation as a composer and teacher that the very invention of counterpoint or concerted music has gravely been attributed to him. Indeed, even at this distance of time, at the end of four hundred years, his name has not lost its Continental reputation : for a French archæologist (M. Stephen Morelot) has recently (in 1856) deciphered and printed two of Dunstable's compositions which he had discovered in the public library at Dijon in Burgundy.

From the beginning of the sixteenth century, down to our own time, the list of English musicians presents an unbroken succession of names.

The last years of the sixteenth and the first of the seventeenth centuries form what might be called the golden age of English music—the age, for all musical Europe, of the Madrigal. Nowhere was the cultivation of that noble form of pure vocal music, whether in composition or performance, followed with more zeal or success than in our own. Our great masters in this branch of art are exactly contemporaneous too with those of Italy,—not subsequent, but exactly contemporaneous.*

With the seventeenth century begins in England, as elsewhere, the third, or transition period of musical history—distinguished by the acceptance of many new principles in musical composition, and by continually increasing skill in many branches of musical practice—instrumental performance especially ; and, more than all, by continually increasing attention to the conformity of notes with words,—in fact the diligent study of everything which goes to perfect what is popularly called " expression" in music.

Attempts, at home as abroad, and not unsuccessful ones, at musical expression, had been made at much earlier epochs ; but no general consciousness of their deficiencies in this respect

---

* Take the two most celebrated in either country—Luca Marenzio and John Wilbye; both of these illustrious musicians were born in or about the year 1555, both died about the end of the century.

prevailed among English musical composers till about the middle of the seventeenth century. Our great poet Milton (himself an excellent musician) has, in the opening of his sonnet to Henry Lawes, who first set the masque of "Comus" to music, sufficiently indicated, within the compass of four lines, what the shortcomings of English composition had been prior to the advent of his friend. He thus addresses him :

> " Harry, whose tuneful and well-measured song
>   First taught our English music how to span
>   Words with just note and accent, not to scan
> With Midas' ears, committing short and long."

From this it is plain that the close alliance of sound and sense to which the musical compositions of Henry Lawes owed their favour was a rarity, even in the middle of the seventeenth century. But assuredly it had been exhibited earlier, though in a form less favourable to expression than that adopted by Lawes, whose best and most numerous compositions are " Ayres" for a single voice.

Two musicians, Dowland and Ford, had, half a century before Lawes, published songs, to be sung either by one voice or by four, which, superior to his in mere musical facture, are scarcely inferior (and this is very high praise) as vehicles for the expression of the words to which they are set. Nor had this particular excellence been unappreciated or unrecognised by the contemporaries of these composers. The name of John Dowland, like that of Henry Lawes, has been enshrined in a poem attributed to a greater even than Milton—Shakspeare. It begins thus :—

> " If music and sweet poetry agree,
>   As needs they must (the sister and the brother),
> Then must the love be great 'twixt thee and me,
>   Because thou lov'st the one, and I the other."

Here the thing taken for granted is that music and poetry, be their characteristics what they may, must of necessity *agree—*

a certain dependence on or subordination to poetry, on the part of music, being implied in their relation as "the sister and the brother." To this agreement, this thorough union and interdependence of words and notes, must be attributed the fact that after two hundred and fifty years some of the compositions of Dowland, and one at least of Ford, "Since first I saw your Face," still retain their popularity. Perhaps no piece of vocal music has been—still is—more often sung than the last I have named.

But their successor Lawes has been less fortunate. Posterity has not confirmed the judgment of Milton in respect to him; and the poet's prophecy—

> "To after years thou shalt be writ the man
> Who with smooth air could'st humour best our tongue,"

is still assuredly unfulfilled. Yet these were not the words of one accustomed to speak from imperfect knowledge or without consideration; and much could be said to justify them. At the time they were written very important experiments were being made, in Italy especially, in musical practice, which, though not attended with the particular results expected by those who made them, contributed greatly towards that change of style by which the music of our own time is distinguished from that of the fifteenth and sixteenth centuries. Milton, as a scholar and a poet, would have watched with interest and with hope the effects of the Renaissance (of which I said so much in my former course) on music. His Italian travels, and his classical tastes, will have led him, as they led far better musicians, to underrate the music of the second period, and to believe that the new style of which he witnessed the growth could be formed without the science by which the old had been so eminently distinguished. The musical declamation of the Greeks—that Philosopher's Stone of our art—had obviously led even his educated taste astray; and at the time the sonnet "to Mr. Henry Lawes" was penned Milton will have entertained—not too great, but—too exclusive an admiration for the "spanning" of—

"Words with just note and accent."

That Lawes achieved this result to perfection, is certain; that he was possessed of a vein of melody quite unprecedented among his countrymen, and still almost unrivalled, is, I think, as certain.   Unfortunately he was an ill-taught musician, unable to develope his own ideas with any effect, or to any good purpose; and he presents another instance of the truth that no lasting popularity has ever been attained for unscientific, ill-constructed music.   A very large number of his compositions are too short and too simple in their plan to betray his musical incapacity.   They are for the most part "Ayres" for a single voice, with a bass not even *figured*,—these Ayres seldom extending beyond a few phrases, or involving more than one or two modulations.   The words he set to music were, almost without exception, interesting, and in most cases beautiful. Two of these Ayres you shall now hear; the first a setting of Waller's well-known Lines to a Lady Singing, "While I listen to thy Voice."   In this may be traced the influence of the then new Italian school founded by Monteverde, and improved by Carissimi.   Lawes had avowedly studied the works of his Italian contemporaries and immediate predecessors, with profound attention.   With some of the same faults, his music exhibits some of the same beauties; and, more than any, that felicitous union of poetical and musical rhythm which makes the sound seem rather a development of the sense than an addition to it; so that words are not so much *sung* to his music as *said* sonorously, and with strict regard to quantity, accent, and (what is generally confounded with it) emphasis.

SONG.—WHILE I LISTEN TO THY VOICE.

The Words by WALLER.   HENRY LAWES.

Parlante.

While I lis - ten to thy voice, Chlo - ris, I feel
my life de - cay; That pow'r - ful noise calls my fleet - ing
soul a - way; O sup - press that ma - gic sound, . .
. . . Which destroys with - out a wound. Peace, peace, Chloris,

peace, or sing - ing die, That to - gether thou and I to heav'n may go; For all we know Of what the bless-ed do a- bove Is that they sing, and that they love.

In his lighter and less ambitious efforts, Lawes is equally careful and equally successful in giving expression to the poetry he takes in hand. Here is a song of a very different character —less fragmentary, and, in one sense, far more musical than that which you have just heard.

SONG.—GO, YOUNG MAN.

Henry Lawes.

Allegretto.

1st v. Go, young man, let my heart a - lone,
2nd v. 'Tis on - ly beau - ty you ad - mire,

'Twill be a pris' - ner un - to none; Nor will I
And that's the ob - ject of de - sire, Which by de-

Cu - pid's shackles wear, Since lo-vers' laws are
grees burns to a flame, And hence Love first re-

so - se - vere. Love is my
ceiv'd its name. Then, young man,

slave whilst I de - spise, But once con - a
give me leave to doubt, Since Love's a

rall.

1st verse. 2nd verse.

tent he'll ty - ran - nize.
fire, and fires .... will out.

If the vocal compositions of Lawes, so interesting in many respects, convey rather an unfavourable impression of English musical science in the first half of the seventeenth century, the instrumental compositions of a contemporary might remove this impression most effectually. John Jenkins, whose only Italian rivals were Frescobaldi and Allegri, actually died, at the age of seventy, fifteen years before any of the compositions of Corelli were given to the world; he may be fairly said, indeed, to have made a reputation, and a great one, before the father of Italian instrumental music was born.

The "Memoires of Musick" of the Hon. Roger North, Attorney-General to James II., a book which, though long known to musical literati in manuscript, was first published only a few years since, through the care of Dr. Rimbault, contains many curious and interesting particulars about this musician, and also about the state of music in England during the first half of the seventeenth century. Any reputation that we may now have among Continental nations, as musicians, must be attributed entirely to our essays in vocal music; in instrumental we must be content to accept a very inferior status. This, however, was certainly not always the case; and many passages could be cited, from foreign as well as English memoirs of the time, to show that, in the composition as well as in the performance of instrumental music, the English were regarded as on the whole superior to any other people. Roger North, for instance, speaking of the Italian *fantazias*, says, "Afterwards these were imitated by the English who, working more elaborately, improved upon their patterne, which gave occasion to an observation, that in vocall, the Italians, and in instrumental music, the English excelled."* And further on he speaks of "those authors whose performances gained to the nation the credit in excelling the Italian in all but the vocall."

* *Memoires of Musick,* pp. 74 and 83.

Another writer of about the same time, Christopher Simpson, says, "You need not seek outlandish authors, especially for instrumental musick; no nation (in my opinion) being equal to the English in that way."[*] And a more positive and pungent authority, Matthew Lock, has the following, "And for those mountebanks of wit, who think it necessary to disparage all they meet with of their own countrymen's, because there have been and are some excellent things done by strangers, I shall make bold to tell them (and I hope my known experience in this science will inforce them to confess me a competent judge) that I never saw any foreign instrumental composition (a few French courantes excepted) worthy an Englishman's transcribing." This is very strong language. But it must be remembered that it was uttered before any of the great Italians who followed shortly after—Corelli, Bassani, Geminiani, Tartini—had given anything to the world, and indeed before some of them had come into it.

I need not say that all the instrumental music of this period, Italian or English, with the partial exception of some of Corelli's, is now utterly forgotten. It will excite no surprise that the writings of John Jenkins have not proved exempt from this common lot. Yet assuredly no composer's reputation could have appeared to be built on a wider or a firmer basis. Jenkins had invention, science, and facility. " For nearly half a century," says North, " the private music in England was, in great measure, supplied by him." Nor was his reputation confined to this country. One at least of his works, a Collection of Sonatas for two Violins and a Bass, was reprinted at Amsterdam (in 1664), and North tells a story (p. 87) of a Spanish Don who " sent some papers to Sir Peter Lely containing one part of an English "Concert," desiring that he would procure and send him the other parts *costa che costa.*" It was shown to Jenkins and recognised

[*] *Compendium of Practical Music,* 1667, p. 145.

by him as from his hand, but when and where he had written
it he was altogether unable to say. Such was the reputation of
this musician at about the middle of the seventeenth century,
that to a contemporary his " Fancies" (the name by which most
of his pieces were known) would have seemed as little likely to go
out of favour as the Quartets of Haydn to any of us. Alas,
for the instability of musical fame! Four bars, forming one poor
little three-part Round, " A Boat, a Boat unto the Ferry," are

all out of the horse-loads of music by John Jenkins which the
world has *not* " willingly let die." Let us devote five minutes
to the payment of a tribute of respect to the memory of this
worthy, and try to find something, in one of his works, of the
charm which so many of them assuredly had for our ancestors.
The piece I have selected for performance, from a collection
which I have here, in a contemporary handwriting, possibly
that of the composer, is one of his Three-Part Fancies. It re-
tains few traces of the old tonality of which I have so often
spoken, and begins and ends in G minor. It is built on two
subjects, not treated at very great length, but certainly with
much skill. It contains a pleasing little episode in triple time
beginning in the relative major key of B ♭. But the most remarkable features of the piece are some chromatic effects which
you will recognise at once, and which you will have some
difficulty in believing to be two hundred years old. I cannot
vouch for their genuineness, though they are unmistakeably
indicated in my old copy. Little reliance is to be placed on
the *accidentals* found in early manuscript music, often inserted,
as they evidently are, by a later hand. In some cases no doubt
such insertion is the verification of a tradition, but in others it is
simply the record of individual fancy.

TRIO.

JOHN JENKINS.

The stream of musical history, which flowed on smoothly in Italy down to the middle of the last century, if not down to our own time, found obstruction in *our* Civil Wars and the social changes which grew out of them, which it cannot be fairly said ever to have thoroughly surmounted. The interdiction of the Choral Service, the dispersion of choirs, and the destruction of organs were, in the middle of the seventeenth century, tantamount to laying the practice of music under an interdict; for be it always remembered, up to this time the best art had been religious art, and the highest genius had hitherto reserved its greatest efforts for the service of the Church. Private musical performance no doubt went on, in a quiet way, during the Protectorate, without interruption or discouragement; indeed the Protector himself was, it is said, a lover of music and might eventually have become a patron of it. But the bolt was shot and could not be recalled, even by the bowman himself.

At the close of the Interregnum, in the year 1660, England might be described as equally wanting in pipes and strings, and in people to play upon them. There were no organs, no organists; voices there were of course, but there were no vocalists. The remedy for this musical famine was, perhaps, inevitable; at all events it would have seemed so to a Court whose tastes and habits were so entirely of foreign growth as that of Charles II. Continental artists must be introduced in considerable numbers; and, to complete our musical denationalization, our young musicians must be sent abroad to learn their art.

Among the first set of choristers got together for the Chapel Royal, after the Restoration, one Pelham Humphreys early attracted attention by his musical aptitude. At this time the works of Lully were regarded by his adopted countrymen, the French, as combining in the most perfect proportions every quality by which music should or could be distinguished. Though some deduction must be made from this national and contemporaneous estimate, Lully was a man of great ability, who had had the good sense or good fortune to form his style on that of Carissimi—unquestionably the greatest genius of the seventeenth century.

By the direction and at the charge of Charles II., Pelham Humphreys was sent to Paris to study under Lully, and like his master therefore *he* formed his style, though at second-hand, on that of Carissimi, and on his return home was the means of making his artistic brethren acquainted with a number of effects, many of them beautiful and all new, and a system of composition differing, in plan and detail, from that of the great English masters of the second period as widely as the " Lyrical Ballads" of Wordsworth differ from the " Pastorals" of Pope.

Before introducing you to an example of Pelham Humphreys' compositions, I will read you one or two passages from a book with which many of you will be familiar, Pepys' Diary, which will serve to introduce to you Pelham Humphreys himself, shortly after his return from the expedition on which he had been sent by Charles II. My attention has been called to these passages by my kind friend Dr. Rimbault, so distinguished for the extent of his reading, especially in English musical history. The passages furnish a lively sketch of the state and progress of post-Restoration music.*

" *Nov.* 22, 1663.—At chapel : I had room in the Privy Seale pew with other gentlemen, and there heard Dr. Killigrew preach. The anthem was good after sermon, being the fifty-first psalme, made for five voices by one of Captain Cooke's boys, a pretty boy. And they say there are four or five of them that can do as much. And here I first perceived that the King is a little

---

* Dr. Rimbault has further obliged me by communicating the following extracts from MSS. in his possession entitled " Moneys received and paid for Secret Services, *Temp. Car. II.*"

1664.—To Pelham Humphreys to defray the charge of his journey into France and Italy, 200*l.*

1665.—To Pelham Humphreys, bounty 100*l.*

1666.—To Pelham Humphreys, bounty 150*l.*

musical, and kept good time with his hand all along the anthem.

" *Nov.* 1, 1667.—To Chapel, it being All Hallows Day, and heard a fine anthem, made by Pelham, who is come over.

" *Nov.* 15, 1667.—Home, and there find, as I expected, Mr. Cæsar and little Pelham Humphreys, lately returned from France, and is an absolute Monsieur, as full of form and confidence and vanity, and disparages everything, and everbody's skill but his own. But to hear how he laughs at all the King's musick here, as Blagrave and others, that they cannot keep time nor tune, nor understand anything; and the Grebus, the Frenchman, the King's master of the music, how he understands nothing, nor can play on any instrument, and so cannot compose; and that he will give him a lift out of his place; and that he and the King are mighty great."

From this last extract we may gather that Master Pelham Humphreys had returned from foreign parts with a very high opinion of his own powers, and a very low one of those of the people among whom he found himself. And this condition of mind he was at no pains to conceal. It is impossible to doubt that his estimate of himself, as well as of the people about him, was a tolerably just one. Of the old English school the last and greatest master, Orlando Gibbons, had been gathered to his fathers forty years before; and its only surviving representatives, Child, Rogers, and a few others, were men advanced in life, whose powers, whatever they might once have been, or have become under more favourable circumstances, had been crippled by years of poverty and neglect, and who found themselves called upon to work under conditions which were new to them and to which they were altogether unequal. In Italy the transition from the style of Palestrina to that of Cavalli, Cesti, and Stradella was made gradually and all but insensibly. But during great part of the time in which it was being made in foreign parts, music, when enjoyed at all in England, was a stolen pleasure, and the only vocal exercise recognised by the law of the land was the practice of unisonous metrical psalmody.

Thus the English music of the first years of the seventeenth century is separated from that of the last by a great gulf, which it was hopeless to expect that those who had been left on its further side should ever bridge over. Those on the near side, therefore, had a clear field before them, and the only impediment to the successful exercise of their invention they were likely to find was the last they would have been likely to take into account— " the weight of too much liberty." Nothing more unlike the ecclesiastical music of any of his English predecessors than that of Pelham Humphreys can possibly be conceived.

Mozart's "Idomeneo" was not a greater advance on all preceding operas, nor Beethoven's " Eroica" on all preceding symphonies, than is the anthem to which I shall now invite you to listen, on all preceding compositions of the same kind. Everything in it was new to English ecclesiastical music—its harmony, melody, and, more than all, plan. In place of the overlapping phrases of the old masters, growing out of one another like the different members of a Gothic tower, we have masses of harmony subordinated to one rhythmical idea; in place of sustained and lofty flights, we have shorter and more timorous ones—these even relieved by frequent halts and frequent divergences; and in lieu of repetition or presentation of a few passages under different circumstances, a continually varying adaptation of music to changing sentiment of words, and the most fastidious observance of their emphasis and quantity. It would be easy to point out the faults in Pelham Humphreys' music, as in all the music of his time, but the faults are at least counterbalanced by the beauties, which were once novelties as well as beauties, and which must ever remain beauties, though to us they may have lost their companion charm.

ANTHEM.—HEAR, O HEAVENS.

Isaiah i. 2, 4, 16, 17, 18.   PELHAM HUMPHREYS.

Hear, . O heav'ns, and give ear, O earth: for the Lord hath spoken. I have nourish'd and brought up chil-dren, and they have re-bell'd against me. Ah! . . sin-ful nation, a seed of e-vil-do-ers,

Ah! sin-ful
children that are corrupters: they have for-sak - en the Lord.

na - tion, they have provok - ed the ho - ly One of Is - ra - el

.... un-to an-ger: Ah! sinful, sin-ful
Ah! sinful nation, Ah! sin-ful

seed of e - vil - do - ers, chil - dren that are cor - rup - ters, they have for-

na - tion.

na - tion.

sak - en the Lord. Ah! sinful nation, Ah! sin - ful na - tion.

Ah! . . . . . . sin - ful na - tion,

Ah! . . . . . . sin - ful na - tion,

sin - ful na - tion, Ah! sin - ful na - - - tion.

sin - ful na - tion, Ah! sin - ful, Ah! . . . . sin-ful na - tion.

sin - ful na - tion, Ah! Ah! sin - ful na - tion.

sin - ful na - tion, Ah! . . . . . sin - ful na - tion.

VERSE.

Put a-way the e - vil of your doings from be - fore mine

Make you clean,

Wash ye,

Soft.

eyes,   seek judgment,

learn to do well,

cease to do e - vil,   re - lieve th' oppressed,

plead,   plead,   plead ..

judge the fa - therless,   for the widow,   for the widow,   plead

for the widow,   for the widow,   plead

·P

.... for the widow.   Come now,   let us reason to-gether, saith the

for   the   widow.   Come now,   let us reason to-gether, saith the

.... for the widow.   Come now,   let us reason to-gether, saith the

Lord,   they shall be   as white as

Lord,   they shall be   as white as

Lord, Tho' your sins   be   as   scar-let,

as scar - let,   they . . . . . shall be   as   wool,

crim - son,   like crim - son,   they shall be   as wool, tho'

crim - son,   like crim - son,   they shall be   as wool, tho'

as scar - let,   they . . . . . shall be as

they be red like crim - son,   like crim - son,   they shall be   as

they be red like crim - son,   like crim - son,   they shall be   as

CHORUS.

Tho' your sins be as scar - - let,

wool. Tho' your sins be as scar - let, they shall be as

wool. Tho' your sins be as scar - let, they shall

CHORUS.

wool. Tho' your sins be as scar - let, they shall be as

FULL.

they shall be as white as snow, tho' they be

white, as white as snow,

be as white, as white as snow, tho' they be red like

white as snow, tho' they be red like

red   like crim - son,   tho' they be red   like crim-son, like

tho' they be red   like   crim - son,   tho' they be   red   like

crim - son,   tho' they be   red   like

crim - son,   tho' they be   red   like crim - son,   red   like

crim - son,   they   shall be   as   wool,   tho' they be

crim - son,   they . . . . shall be as   wool,

crimson,   they shall   be   as   wool, tho' they be red   like

crim - son,   they shall   be   as   wool, tho' they be red   like

red like crim - son, tho' they be red like

tho' they be red like crim - son, tho' they be

crim - son, tho' they be

crim - son, tho' they be red like crim - son,

crim-son, like crim - son, they shall be as wool.

red like crim - son, they . . . . shall be as wool.

red like crim-son, they shall be as wool.

red like crim - son, they shall be as wool.

Pelham Humphreys' career as a composer is the very shortest on record. It extends over something less than seven years. He returned from Paris in 1667, and died in 1674, at the early age of twenty-seven. Yet no artist ever exercised a greater influence on his age and country; none so great an influence within so short a space of time. It may be traced in the compositions of his fellow-students Wise and Blow—men of his own standing; in those of Purcell, who was but sixteen years old at the time Humphreys died; and in the still later compositions of Croft, Weldon, and others of inferior mark,—in fact in the writings of every English composer educated before the arrival of Handel in England, in 1710.

In the works of three of the musicians I have just named, Blow, Wise, and Purcell, there is a strong family likeness; although those of the last, Purcell, are distinguished by far greater originality, strength, and sweetness. In all, as there are some of the same excellences, so there are some of the same faults. If they now and then reach the sublime in expression, they sometimes make the one step beyond it. They often follow the changing sense of the words, to the sacrifice of everything like musical construction. Their themes are rarely developed to any considerable extent: their movements rarely comprise more than a few phrases, which do not, as I just said, grow out of one another, like those of the old and of the best modern masters, but are rather patched on to one another, often in a somewhat inconsequent manner.

I have more than once called attention to the fact that many musical forms and effects now indispensable to musical practice were, up to the end of the sixteenth century, only used by a few composers, and used only by them in a somewhat tentative and very reticent way. The most striking of these is the " perfect cadence," a figure so familiar to nineteenth century ears that it is hard to believe it formed no part of the composer's recognised material up to about two hundred and fifty years ago, and that before the seventeenth century it was not an accepted, but rather a discredited and tabooed, form. In the second half of the seventeenth century every trace of that hesitation had been removed. In the works of Carissimi it is at least of sufficiently frequent occurrence, but in those of his imitators it recurs literally *ad nauseam.* They seem to have been never weary of using it.

In an anthem by Michael Wise, a very popular one, "Prepare ye the Way of the Lord," there are in the first movement, which consists of only fourteen bars, no less than six perfect cadences, in the direct or uninverted form ; the composition, which consists in all of but ninety-seven bars, being actually broken up into no less than eight movements. In an anthem by Jeremiah Clarke, " Praise the Lord, O Jerusalem !" which is of about the same length as this of Wise, and which is divided into six movements, the time undergoes no less than five changes. As to the perfect cadences, they are introduced in every second bar.

Moreover, a very serious error of taste first made its appearance about this time, no sign of which I discern in the writings of Humphreys, but which disfigures some, and some too of the best, works of the greatest of his successors, Purcell. This, which shows itself in an extravagance of expression which amounts almost to musical *punning,* arises from a very false though not uncommon view both of the powers and the purposes of music. Music is a highly suggestive, but not an imitative, art. Musicians have at times lost sight of this truth ; and, misled by certain seeming analogies, they have turned the powers of sound to improper uses, and not content with portraying or suggesting by particular successions of notes particular states of feeling, they have tried to mimic the actions of man and the lower animals, and even the changing appearances of inanimate nature.

Two examples will sufficiently illustrate my meaning. Purcell, generally so very felicitous, so true to nature and art, in his expression, opens his anthem, "They that go down to the Sea in Ships," by a descending musical passage of two octaves, thus :—

And a little further on he presents us with the words, "They are carried up to heaven and down again to the deep," as follows :—

Now I do not think there is any true analogy between "going down to the sea" and going down the scale; between being "carried up to heaven" by the force of the winds and waves, and being carried up to the top of one's voice by any influence whatever. Nor is there any obvious resemblance between the fearful chasms of a rolling sea—the "deep," as it is finely called in the Scriptures—and a very exceptional and often ludicrous note at the bottom of a bass voice. If there be any analogy, or similitude, or parity between these several actions and things, and the passages I have sung, it follows that there is analogy, or similitude, or parity among the things themselves : for "things equal to the same thing are equal to one another."

But enough of the faults and shortcomings of these composers, faults in defence of which much might be said, and which, admitted in full, amount to very little, and are the all but inevitable result of the circumstances in which they found themselves placed. Let us return to the more agreeable occupation of contemplating their beauties, exhibited as they are, in the greatest number and to the greatest advantage, in the works of Henry Purcell.

Of the life of this, the most interesting of English musicians, but few particulars have been preserved. Purcell has to be added to the list of those illustrious musicians who have justified the apophthegm, " Those whom the gods love, die young." His career ended with his thirty-eighth year ; but, happily for the world, it was begun early. He was admitted to the Chapel Royal as a probationer at six years of age, immediately after the death of his father, from whom, probably, he received his first instructions in music ; and, before the termination of his occupation as a choir-boy, *i.e.*, before his fifteenth year, he had actually made a considerable reputation as a composer in the highest and most difficult branch of composition, Church music. His first musical impressions will have been received through the works of Pelham Humphreys who, you will remember, returned from Paris in 1667, when Purcell would have been nine years of age. Shortly after Humphreys' return, Cooke, the first master of the boys subsequently to the Restoration, on whom had devolved the difficult task of reconstructing the Royal Choir, died, and Humphreys reigned in his stead. As a matter of course Purcell became his pupil, and was early made familiar with that new style of which I have spoken so often. Purcell, like every man of great genius, was to a great extent self-taught. His Church music more especially indicates acquaintance with a larger, more learned, and therefore earlier, style than that on which Humphreys had formed his. It is well known that at this time all such music—all the works of our old masters—had been consigned to the Index Expurgatorius of King Charles II. That " brisk and airy

Prince," tolerant of so many other things, was altogether in-
tolerant of the ancient modes, of contrapuntal artifice and, as
an old Editor puts it, of " the grave and solemn way which had
been established by Tallis, Byrd, and others." His majesty liked
music " to which he could beat time;" thus measuring it, in
more senses than one, by a rule of thumb. But though the
grave and solemn way might be tabooed, much of the music in
which it had been followed had escaped destruction. The old
books, the depositories of the learning and genius of his predecessors, were still accessible to, and doubtless often opened by,
Henry Purcell. One can picture to oneself this gifted and
beautiful boy piecing together from half a dozen separate part
books (scores were rare in those days) some of these venerable
Services and Anthems, and trying to realize, with his mind's
ear, something of the effect of that music in which a Henry VIII.
might have taken part, and by which an Elizabeth or a Charles I.
might have worshipped within those very walls in which they
were still housed; and, though of course not unsusceptible
to the influences of his own time, wondering over the chances
and changes which had for the moment reduced all this to the
value of waste paper, and revolving the possibility, not of galva-
nizing into a ghastly and ridiculous caricature of existence that
of which the life had long been extinct and the work long done,
but of turning to account the eternal principles of truth and
beauty which had once quickened it, in a style of music which,
whether better or worse, was the only style acceptable to his
own generation. This, so far as one can read his mind in his
works, Purcell must have aimed at; and this, to a considerable
extent, he succeeded in attaining to. In his secular works no
less than in his ecclesiastical, in his instrumental compositions
no less than in his vocal, there is a strength, a clearness, a
healthiness which, though never manifested in a revival of the
sustained grandeur of the old Italian and English schools, or
an anticipation of that of the modern German school—for at

the time in which his lot was cast that was impossible—there
is, I say, in all his writings that which only the discipline
attendant on the study of music of a very different epoch to
that of his own could possibly have given to them.

We have neither time nor force now to justify all this or anything like it, by illustration ; but in the, with one exception,
minor compositions of this great composer which you will now
hear, all of which I have extracted from his secular works,
you will, I think, discern irrefragable evidence of a rich vein
of melody, of a fine taste in harmony, of a delicate sense both
of the inward graces and the outward signs of poetry ;—all
these powers made orderly and effective by that science which
in the works of great artists, though often occult, is never
altogether inoperative, or undiscernible by the inquiring eye
or ear. The one composition to which I have alluded, which
cannot be called minor, is the song, " You Twice Ten Hundred
Deities," which, like many other of Purcell's single songs, forms
part, not of an opera but, of a play, " The Indian Queen," a
joint production of Dryden and Sir Robert Howard. I find
that this play was first produced in 1665, when Purcell was
only seven. It is impossible to believe that the music you are
about to hear can have been the production of a youth of that
age, or indeed of any Englishman at so early a date. It bears
all the traces both of a very practised hand and of a later time,
and must belong to Purcell's mature years.

In the same play, "The Indian Queen," is another song of very
different character, " I attempt from Love's Sickness to fly,"
which will remind those who were present at my first lecture of a
song by Cavalli ; seeing that, though the details are different in
every respect, the form—the Rondo form as it might be called,
wherein the first subject is repeated after every section—is
adopted in both. It has always been regarded as one of the
most touching and refined of Purcell's compositions.

SCENE.—YOU TWICE TEN HUNDRED DEITIES.

From "*The Indian Queen.*"   H. PURCELL.

Recitativo.

You twice ten hundred De - i-ties, to whom, to whom we daily

sa - cri-fice; Ye pow'rs, ye pow'rs that dwell with Fates be-

cres.

low, And see what Men are doom'd to do; Where Elements in

dis - - - - - - - - - cord dwell; Thou, God of sleep, a-

rise - - - - - and tell, Tell, great Zempoalla, what strange, strange fate

cres.

must on her dis - - - - - mal, dis - - mal vi - sion wait.

AIR.
Moderato. ($\stackrel{\frown}{}$ = 80.)

By the croaking of the

p

Toad, In her cave that makes a - bode;

By the croaking of the Toad, In her cave that makes a - bode;

Earthy Dun, Earthy Dun that pants . . . . . .

. . . . for breath, With her swell'd . . . . . .

cres.

sides full, full, full . . . . of death;

f

By the Death's head on thy back; By the twist - - -

- - - ed Serpents plac'd For a

girdle round . . . . thy waist; By the

cres. *f* *p*

hearts of gold that deck thy breast, thy shoulders, and thy neck;

p

mu - sic keep, that us'd to lull thee, us'd to lull thee,

lull thee in thy sleep.

That us'd to lull thee, lull thee, lull thee, us'd to

lull thee, lull thee in thy sleep.

AIR.—I ATTEMPT FROM LOVE'S SICKNESS TO FLY.

From "*The Indian Queen.*" H. PURCELL.

Andante Grazioso. (♩ = 92.)

I at-tempt from Love's sick-ness to fly . . . . in vain, Since I am my-self my own fe-ver, Since I am my-self my own fe-ver and pain. No more now, no more now, fond heart, with pride no more swell, Thou

As it has been one of my objects, throughout these lectures, to introduce you to some composers with whom you might have had little previous acquaintance, so of others whose names are generally better known I have been careful to bring under your notice only such compositions as have not, I think, received their fair share of attention. It would be easy to follow this latter course in respect to Purcell. He presents no exception to the general industry and versatility of great musical composers. We rise from the perusal of a list of his productions, wondering alike at its extent and variety. His sacred music alone, as scientific and as highly finished as it is original and interesting, fills, in a recent edition, four large and closely-printed volumes ; his instrumental music, which has never been collected, would probably occupy still more space ; he wrote many operas, not mere strings of songs, but veritable operas, in which the business of the drama is for the most part worked out in music ; and he contributed a large quantity of incidental music, vocal and instrumental, to the plays written, or revived with alterations, by Davenant, Dryden, and others.

From this vast repertory I shall choose two, not of the least but of the best-known pieces—pieces forming now accepted portions of one of the most familiar of Shakspeare's dramas, " The Tempest." A specimen or two of Purcell's illustrations of Shakspeare will not be inappropriate to the present time :* perhaps it would be hard to find a time to which they would be. They are all utterances of the same personage, the loveliest of poetical creations, the " delicate Ariel." Surely if ever musician had ear to catch, memory to retain, and hand to record any of those " noises" of which Prospero's isle was " full," those

" Sounds and sweet airs that give delight and hurt not,"

Purcell was he.

* That of the Tercentenary Commemoration of the Poet's birth.

AIR AND CHORUS.—FULL FATHOM FIVE.

From Shakespear's "*Tempest.*"

H. Purcell.

Full fa - thom five thy fa - ther

lies; Full fa - thom

five thy fa - ther lies; Of his bones is co - - - ral made; Those are

AIR AND CHORUS.—COME UNTO THESE YELLOW SANDS.

From SHAKESPEAR'S "*Tempest.*" H. PURCELL.

LECTURE VI.

ENGLAND—continued.

HANDEL—HIS EDUCATION—ZACKAU—HAMBURG—KEISER—
"THE PASSION" — ITALY — ENGLAND — " RINALDO"—
WATER MUSIC—THE DUKE OF CHANDOS—"ACIS AND
GALATEA"—SUBJECTS AND TREATMENT—CHAMBER DUET,
"DAGL' AMORI"—INSTRUMENTAL MUSIC—THE HARPSI-
CHORD — PIÈCES POUR LE CLAVECIN — COURANTE —
"SOSARME"—" SEMELE"—CONCLUSION.

LECTURE VI.

ENGLAND—CONTINUED.

I ENDEAVOURED to show, in my last Lecture, to what extent the Italian music of the Transition Period had influenced our own. The traditions of the English School had been broken off by the Civil Wars; and that great change of style which came over the music of other countries gradually and spontaneously, had to be made in our own suddenly, and under exotic influences. Our first great composer, after the Restoration, Henry Purcell, received his earliest musical impressions from Pelham Humphreys, a pupil of Lully, who, in his turn, had formed his style on that of Carissimi—indisputably the type of the Transition Period—the composer whose works at once surpass and, as it were, resume all others of his age.

The style of music imported by Pelham Humphreys, and adopted by his fellow-students Wise and Blow, and subsequently developed by Purcell, and Purcell's successors; Croft, under whose hand English music seemed for a time to be resuming its wonted masculine character; Jeremiah Clarke, whose grace and sensibility all but redeemed his want of science; John Weldon, perhaps the most tasteful ecclesiastical composer we have yet had;—in fact, the style of every English composer whose education had been completed before the year 1710, continued in favour for about half a century.

In the month of December of that year George Frederick Handel made his first visit to England. This visit proved even more fruitful in results than that of Humphreys to

R

France; for not only did it again change the character of English music, but it added one of the greatest of German names to the list of *English* composers.

The details of Handel's life are so easily accessible, and indeed so extensively known, that I shall only mention a few dates in connexion with some of them, in order to make what I have to say about the development of his genius intelligible.

He was born at Halle in Saxony in 1685. Like most other great musicians, he exhibited his aptitude, and what is so often mistaken for it his liking, for music, very early; but his father, who was a doctor of medicine, opposed the cultivation of his particular taste most strongly; as, by the way, the father of every man of genius is invariably said to have done. Fortunately for the world, certain accidents served to remove Dr. Handel's scruples, and his son was placed under the instruction of Zackau, an excellent contrapuntist and skilful organ player. Handel was "an old man's child:" his father had attained the age of sixty-three when his son was born to him. It is not astonishing therefore that the latter was left fatherless at an early age. Dr. Handel died, at the age of seventy-five, when his son was in his thirteenth year. For some time, though with occasional interruptions, the young Handel continued to profit by the instruction and assistance of Zackau; but at the age of eighteen, doubtless furnished with more science and skill than judgment and taste, but strong in hope and not wanting in self-reliance, he set off, with a light heart and a lighter purse, like some hero of a fairy tale, to seek his fortune. Of course he was not long in reaching the gates of an Enchanter's palace, the doors of which yielded willingly to the "open Sesame" which he bore about with him. This palace was the Hamburg Theatre, and the Enchanter that very Reinhard Keiser about whom I said a good deal in my third Lecture, and of whose powers of enchantment you then had an opportunity of forming some estimate. At this time Keiser, Handel's senior by twelve years, had made some way in the long and splendid career which proved to be before him, and had more than begun to exercise that influence which subsequently made itself felt so actively and so widely. He was "facile princeps" among the musicians, not of his age perhaps, but of his country. Among those of his own standing he had no doubt many equals in contrapuntal skill and general knowledge; but in invention, facility, and taste, he stood alone among his compatriots. J. S. Bach, like Handel (they were born in the same year), was as yet, at the time of which I am speaking, among those always uncertain and often disappointing personages—promising young men.

Among Keiser's forces Handel then enrolled himself, in the comparatively humble capacity of a "ripieno," second violin. The tide which leads on to fortune was not long in rising to his feet, nor he unready to take it at the flood. The sudden indisposition, not of the Prima Donna nor even of the Primo Tenore, but of the Clavecinist, gave him an opportunity of which he was in every sense prepared to avail himself. The duties of the Clavecinist, up to a time quite recent, in an opera performance, were both onerous and delicate. The greater part of the dialogue was delivered in recitative, not accompanied as is now the custom by more or less of the whole orchestra, but by a single Violoncello, Double Bass, and Harpsichord; and even of Songs large portions were left with no other written accompaniment than a figured bass, out of which the Clavecinist was expected to call into existence graces innumerable,—thus in the fullest sense

> " Untwisting all the chains that tye
> The hidden soul of Harmony."

Handel's temporary lieutenancy soon led to permanent and recognised occupation, and the substitute became a responsible officer. Nor was his faculty for composition long without an opportunity of being tested.. During his stay in Hamburg he produced four operas, which proved, with two or three exceptions, to be the only works with German words he ever set to music. To one of these exceptions 1 have now to call your special attention. It is "The Passion," according to St. John; interesting, if for no other reason, as the earliest work of Handel that has been preserved (it is anterior to any even of the operas I have just named), but far more so as exhibiting his first manner; thus enabling us to estimate the effect which his subsequent travels in Italy, and residence in England, had upon his taste and genius.

This very curious work was first given to the world only a year or two since—a century and a half after its completion and first performance. Its publication is due to the German Handel Society, of whose noble edition of Handel's complete works it forms Part IX. The editor, Herr Chrysander, tells us, in his brief preface, that it "bears so genuine a Handelian impress, that, notwithstanding its youthful immaturity, it may claim a place in the series of Handel's works on its own account," and that "no one will think of doubting its Handelian origin." That it may claim a place among Handel's works on its own account, that is as a work of genius, and one which those who have gone into its history are fully satisfied is Handel's, is unquestionable. But that "no one will think of doubting its Handelian origin," from internal evidence, is so far from being the case that I cannot discern in it the slightest trace of that manner with which the subsequent works of Handel—even the earliest of these—are unmistakeably impressed. The external or historical evidence of the work being Handel's would seem to be very strong indeed; but the internal has, it seems to me, been excogitated by the learned Editor "from the depths of his own moral consciousness." Had the work been brought under my notice anonymously, I should, I hope, have been able to fix its date pretty accurately, but I should have hesitated long in assigning it to any particular author. It abounds in passages, or rather turns of expression, which are not unfrequent in the works of J. S. Bach, but which are not at all peculiar to him; while the vocal parts are far more becoming to the voice than any Bach ever wrote, except by accident. The work is one that none but a singer could have written; and Handel, we know, though he had but a feeble voice, sang so exquisitely as to have given pleasure to the greatest vocalists of his own time—eminently a time of great vocalists.

The pieces to which I shall now ask you to listen form an uninterrupted series, beginning with the work itself. They lose something, as all music does, by the translation of the words to which it is set, however skilfully that may be made; but for this you will make allowance. The work begins with a short symphony followed by a recitative for a Tenor voice, to which the part of the Evangelist is assigned throughout. This recitative is followed by a song for a Soprano, which I am sure you will agree in thinking exquisite. It contains too the only quasi-Handelian passage in the selection. The first phrase bears some resemblance to that of the opening of the beautiful quintet, " All that is in Hamor mine," in Handel's " Jephtha" —his last oratorio, which is thus connected with his first by a cycle of labour extending over all but fifty years. This song is followed by another Tenor recitative, and a chorus; this again by another Tenor recitative, and this by a short Alto air for Pilate, to whom some of the most graceful, I would almost say some of the most touching, passages in the work are assigned. We will stop with a duet for two Sopranos, which is perhaps the most interesting movement of all. It is full of " imitation," the first six bars indeed being in strict canon in unison. It concludes with a most striking effect (evidently called forth by the words) which the composer has thrown into the instrumental bass, the vocal melody remaining undisturbed— gliding on like the waters of some deep clear stream, over and round about some great boulder which has tumbled into its bed.

THE PASSION.

John xix.

Handel (1704).

stain, To the pure and righteous Sa - viour,

to the Sa - viour, Are a weight of care far

beavier, a weight far hea - vier, Than the

cru - el scourge's pain, ... Than the cru - el scourge's

pain.   Thee, O

man . . . .   Thee, O   man . . . .

. . . the thought a - bash - es,   the thought a - bash - es, God for

thee endures these lashes,   God for thee en - dures these

lash - es, Thee, O

man, the thought a - bashes, God for thee endures these lash - es, God for

thee en - dures these lash - es.

RECIT. (TENOR.)

And the sol - diers stripped him, and platt - ed a crown of thorns, and

put it up-on his head, and put on him a purple robe, and said,

CHORUS.
Allegro.

King of Ju-dah! King of Ju-dah! Hail! all hail to thee!

King of Ju-dah! King of Ju-dah! Hail! all hail to thee!

King of Ju-dah! King of Ju-dah! Hail! all hail to thee!

King of Ju-dah! King of Ju-dah! Hail! all hail to thee!

King of Ju-dah! King of Ju-dah! Hail! all hail to thee!

RECIT. (TENOR.)

And with their hands they smote him. Pi-late therefore went forth a-

AIR. (ALTO.)
Andante.

gain, and saith un - to them: (PILATE.) Be - hold! Be-

hold! I bring him forth to you, that ye may

know that I find no fault, I find no fault . .

RECIT. (TENOR.)

Then came Je-sus forth, wearing the crown of thorns, and pur-ple robe.

DUET. (SOPRANI.)
Adagio non troppo.

See our lov'd Je - sus is like to the ro - ses,

See our lov'd Je - sus is like to the

Yet he is lov - li - er far than the bush - es Which the fair

Yet he is lov - li - er far than the bush - es

mea - dows, which the fair Je - richo's mea - dows a - dorn;

Which the fair mea - dows, fair Je - richo's mea - dows a - dorn;

For the deep wounds of our sins he will che - rish,

For the deep wounds of our sins he will che - rish,

Tend - ed by him we ne - ver shall pe - rish, For the deep

Tend - ed by him we ne - ver shall pe - rish, For the deep

wounds of our sins he will che - rish, For the deep wounds of our

wounds of our sins he will che - rish, For the deep wounds of our

sins he will che - rish, Tend - ed by him we ne - ver shall

sins he will che - rish, Tend - ed by him we ne - ver shall

S

pe - rish.

pe - rish.

Handel's stay in Hamburg lasted three years at the end of which, in 1706, at the age of twenty-one, having had much experience in practical composition, and some in the superintendence of operatic performance, he turned his steps in the direction towards which his thoughts had doubtless been long inclined—to Italy.

I have said enough already about the attractions which the South of Europe must have held out to a young and inquiring musician born on this side of the Alps, in the first years of the eighteenth century. In 1706–9, which were the years occupied by Handel's Italian travels, Alessandro Scarlatti was at the summit of his reputation. The majority of the best pupils of the school which he founded—the Neapolitan—were mere youths; but one or two, his son Domenico, for instance, and Porpora, were already distinguished artists. Corelli was still living at Rome, in the enjoyment of the dignity which attends on the last years of a long and useful life, and his pupil Geminiani was carrying further the principles and practices which Corelli had done so much to establish and improve. Venice, never behind, generally ahead of, the rest of Italy in artistic culture, abounded in excellent musicians, among whom Lotti was the most complete, and Marcello the most promising. Gasparini, Steffani, and Clari were all in the fullest exercise of their powers. In Rome too, so rich in traditions of all kinds, those of the old masters, notwithstanding their rapid decay elsewhere, were still preserved and passed on, with jealous and reverential care; the music of Palestrina was still worthily performed, and the style which he had perfected still lived in the fresh productions of Tomaso Bai and Giuseppe Pitoni.

Then, again, the most fascinating of musical arts—the art of singing—new even in Italy, was absolutely unknown elsewhere. To one with dispositions like Handel's who had never heard anything better than the vocal utterances of his compatriots, which one of their own old writers on music has likened to the howling of wolves,—to one, I say, who had never heard anything better than German singing, the spontaneous utterance, the smooth passage from note to note, the flexibility, the sweetness and strength, to say nothing of the sentiment, of an Italian singer of the eighteenth century, would have been not so much a sensation more delightful than any he had ever known before, as the revelation and first experience of some new sense.

It follows too that the people among whom artists like those I have named were living and working—had been living and working for more than a century and a half—had had their susceptibility to beauty—to musical beauty especially—developed to the highest conceivable point, and that a musical student would find in Italy not merely excellent individual models and

s 2

instructors, but an atmosphere in which, if even unconsciously, he would inhale music at every pore.

To realize the effect of all these influences upon one so prepared for them as Handel—prepared by his sterling musical science and skill, no less than by his susceptibility and his youth—no great effort of imagination would be needed, even were all evidence in respect to it wanting. Fortunately this is not the case; for we have the best of all evidence of this effect—nothing less than that of his subsequent life and works. Those three years in Italy transformed, or rather re-formed, him entirely; and the Handel who returned to Germany in 1709, returned with new aspirations, new tastes, new methods of working—returned, in fact, a new man; for with artists " the style is the man."

In 1709, I say, Handel returned to Germany—not, however, to his native place, or to the place of his apprenticeship, but to Hanover, where the Elector received him with open arms; for the young composer had made some reputation during his travels, having given something to, in exchange for what he had brought away from, Italy. The Elector offered him the position of Chapel Master in his Court, and what was in those days a handsome salary. This offer he accepted, on condition of being allowed such leave of absence as would enable him to visit England, which some English nobleman with whom he fell in at Hanover had invited him to do. He reached London in the month of December, 1710. He was not many days in our busy capital before a commission was given him, to set to music an opera called "Rinaldo," founded on a well-known episode of Tasso's " Jerusalem Delivered," the libretto of which was the work of Aaron Hill, a small contemporary poet, who was then also manager of the Haymarket Theatre. Hill of course wrote his drama in English, and it was translated into Italian by a certain Giacomo Rossi. Handel's rapidity of composition would seem to have driven this poor man nearly frantic. He proved quite unable to keep pace with the young, inventive and practised musician, who set his verses to music faster than he had written them, and who unceasingly taxed the poet's invention and industry for "more copy." Rossi has left a record of his collaboration with Handel, in a short and not ungraceful preface to the printed copy of the work.

"Accept, I pray thee, discreet reader (he says), this my hurried labour, and if it should not prove worthy of thy praise, do not at any rate refuse it thy compassion—I would rather say, thy justice—having regard to my limited time ; inasmuch as the Signor Handel, the Orpheus of our age, in putting it to music, has hardly given me time to write, far less to think; for, I have in the present instance been the amazed witness of an unprecedented feat—the composition of an opera, complete and perfect in all its parts, in the incredibly short space of fourteen days !"

In fourteen days, or rather within fourteen days, then, according to this amazed witness, Handel threw off an opera, by no means inconsiderable even in respect to quantity, the vigour, sweetness, originality, and science of which at once established his reputation in England. It was played many times successively, to the exclusion of every other opera. Its reputation soon spread to the Continent, and its success was as great in the principal theatres of Italy and Germany as in London. It was this work that called forth Handel's *bon mot*, addressed to Walsh the publisher, who, it was said, had cleared 1500*l.* by it. " My good sir, as it is right we should be upon an equal footing, *you* shall compose the next opera, and *I* will sell it."

Of all Handel's works " Rinaldo," though of course not the greatest, is surely the most interesting ; for it was his first considerable production after his return northwards from Italy. In comparing a few specimens of it, therefore, with those you heard just now, of " The Passion," written, you will remember, before he left Germany, you will have the best possible opportunity of testing the truth of what I have said—that his Italian travels entirely changed his style.

It will be objected perhaps that no fair comparison is possible between an oratorio or Church cantata and an opera. But it must be remembered that Handel came to England in the capacity, professed and acknowledged, of an opera composer; and that it was not till three years after his first visit that he gave his adopted countrymen any opportunity of judging of his talent as an Ecclesiastical musician, by the composition of the Utrecht "Te Deum" and "Jubilate;" while his second attempt at oratorio was delayed till the year 1717, when he wrote, at Hanover, his second "Passion"—thirteen years after the first. *This* work, I may observe in passing, though set to German words, is as widely different from the first, in style, as any two works of the same class by any two different composers that could possibly be named. Moreover, by the time Handel set the Utrecht " Te Deum," a new influence had been exercised upon him— that of English music. No doubt any setting of the " Te Deum" by Handel would have been a fine one; but it would surely have been altogether unlike the Utrecht, had he never seen Purcell's—which he has followed closely, even to a fault. Handel's style subsequently to his Italian tour must therefore be judged by his secular works, since there are no others to test it by, of the same date.

I will ask you therefore to listen to three pieces—the first two the songs, " Lascia ch'io pianga" and " Il Tricerbero ;" the last, a march.

I have read somewhere that the former of these songs is founded on an instrumental movement—a " minuet" in fact— written by Handel many years before. It may be so. Somebody may have danced to this tune before it left Hamburg, but it is more certain that many have wept to it since it came back from Italy.

Of a very different class is the latter, to which more than one set of English words of a bacchanalian character have been adapted. The subject of the original is the victory of Rinaldo, the hero of the drama, over the three-headed monster, Cerberus.

AIR.—LASCIA CH'IO PIANGA.

From the Opera "*Rinaldo.*"

HANDEL.

li - ber - tà.

Il duolo in - fran - ga

Fine.

ques - te ri - tor - te, De miei mar - ti - ri sol per pie-

tà.. De miei mar - ti - ri sol per pie - tà.

SONG.—IL TRICERBERO UMILIATO.

From the Opera "*Rinaldo.*" HANDEL (1711).

... dò, Al mio bran - do, Al mio bran-do ren-de-

rò, ... ren - de - rò, .. Al mio

bran - do ren - de - rò!

A short instrumental movement in this opera attained, and for many years maintained, the most extraordinary popularity—the "March." It was adopted by the regiment of Life Guards who, it is said, played it every day upon parade for forty years. And, twenty years after its first production, it was arranged by Pepusch, as a song and chorus in "The Beggar's Opera," and sung to the following words:—

> " Let us take the road;
> Hark, I hear the sound of coaches,
> The hour of attack approaches;
>   T'your arms, brave boys, and load.
>   See the ball I hold;
> Let the chemists toil like asses,
> Our fire their fire surpasses,
>   And turns our lead to gold !"

MARCH.

From the Opera " *Rinaldo.*"

HANDEL.

Handel remained in London for six or seven months after the production of his opera "Rinaldo," and then returned to Hanover. The small capital of a small German State proved but an unexciting residence to one who had finished a sort of royal progress through Europe by a splendid reception in London. Obtaining a new leave of absence, he reappeared in London, in January, 1712, not many months after he had quitted it. Here he remained, the centre of a continually increasing circle of friends and admirers, altogether unmindful of the duties of his office at Hanover (which he still held), until they were suddenly and somewhat alarmingly brought to his recollection by the arrival in England of the Elector, who, on the death of Queen Anne, became King George I. Handel, who, it must be admitted, had treated his old master very ill, was naturally doubtful how far the King might resent his neglect and insubordination. He therefore kept out of his Majesty's way till some favourable occasion might present itself for making his apologies and his peace. A certain Baron Kilmanseck succeeded in finding this. The King attending a fête on the river Thames, Handel prepared a number of short instrumental pieces, which the Baron arranged should be played in a barge which followed that of the King, who very soon, it is said, finding out to whose strains he was listening, not unwillingly restored Handel, shortly after, to his favour.

This succession of little pieces is known, from the occasion which suggested the composition and first performance of them, as Handel's "Water Music." They are scored for, besides the usual stringed instruments, flutes, oboes, bassoons, trumpets, and French horns. The introduction of this latter instrument (now a *sine quâ non* in the orchestra) must have been a great novelty at this time. I wish you could hear one or two of these very elegant movements in their original orchestral form, but even from the pianoforte arrangement which I have made you will be quite able to understand the clemency of King George I. to his penitent composer.

AIR.

From the "*Water Music.*"   HANDEL.

George I., whatever may have been his shortcomings in other respects, certainly knew good music when he heard it, and how to take care of a good musical composer when he had found—in this instance, recovered—him. Having occasion in 1716 to revisit Hanover, his Majesty, who certainly had proved the truth of the proverb, "out of sight out of mind," determined to take Handel with him. The king and the composer passed the year 1717 in Hanover. On their return to England, the latter took up his residence with a nobleman whose wealth, taste, and munificence have earned him the title accorded three centuries before to Lorenzo de' Medici. For "the magnificent" Duke of Chandos some of the best Church and Chamber music of Handel's earlier years was composed, and among the latter the exquisite pastoral " Acis and Galatea." Handel had already composed and produced a Cantata on this same subject, at Naples, in 1708; but, with trifling exceptions, the English " Acis" is an altogether different work. This was first produced at Cannons, the residence of the Duke of Chandos, in 1720, laid aside, and probably forgotten by the composer, till the year 1732, when it was performed, possibly without his consent, certainly without his participation, and at last reproduced (with many additions) under his own direction.

" Acis and Galatea," however, did not assume its present shape till many years after this. Once revived, the world would not willingly part with it a second time; and it was subsequently often performed under the direction of the composer, who—as was his wont—made additions to, subtractions from, and alterations in it, for every performance.

Whether from pressure of time, or from a very natural unwillingness that so much good material and careful workmanship should be wasted, Handel often fell back, later in life, on the productions of his earlier years. And this, in two ways. (1) He took the "subjects" of former compositions, and treated them in a new way, developing them more fully, decorating them, and augmenting their interest by the addition of others; and (2) a much more simple procedure, he took his older compositions bodily, and adapted them to new situations and to new words— often of a very different character.

The former of these procedures is one of the commonest possible among musicians. The genius and science of a great master are exhibited so much more signally in the treatment of the subjects of a large movement—such a one, for instance, as " We never will bow down," in " Israel in Egypt," or the "Amen" chorus in "The Messiah"—than in the subjects themselves, that musicians have at all times felt themselves justified, not merely in making the same passages the subjects of different compositions, but in using as subjects passages *not* of their own invention.

T 2

In the early ages of modern music, *i.e.*, in the fifteenth and sixteenth centuries, this practice was rather the rule than the exception; and even much later times might present us with examples of structures of surpassing grandeur reared on old foundations, or whose walls held many a stone which had done duty elsewhere.

Thus—to bring in evidence one of the most inventive as well as one of the most learned of modern composers—the principal subjects of Mozart's overture to " Die Zauberflöte" and of his finale to the " Jupiter" symphony are, both of them, to be found in the " Forty-eight Fugues" of J. S. Bach,—who, again, was certainly not the inventor of the latter, nor perhaps of the former. More recently, entire operas have been built up on national melodies,—in two instances on one melody each. Take away "Robin Adair" from Boildieu's "La Dame Blanche," or " The Last Rose of Summer" from Flotow's " Martha," with the passages which grow directly or indirectly out of them, and both those popular operas would cease to have visible or audible existence.

As to Handel, like every composer of his own time, he would have used old subjects—whether his own or not—without the faintest idea ever crossing his mind that he was palming off old goods for new ones, or stealing other people's. I dwell longer than might at first seem necessary on these reproductions and so called " plagiarisms," because a good deal has been said about them lately. One of Handel's most recent biographers, M. Schœlcher, has wasted much excellent indignation, and poured out many vials of wrath on certain musical critics who have indicated the movements in which Handel has availed himself of the labours of his predecessors and contemporaries. Heedless of the danger of proving too much, M. Schœlcher would seem to claim for Handel the invention of every passage to be found in the many works which bear his name—a claim which could not be substantiated in respect to the most inventive genius the world has ever seen.

In one instance which "Acis and Galatea" presents of adaptation of old materials, Handel has achieved a feat analogous to what builders call " under-pinning." He has not furbished up an old fabric with a new façade, nor has he rebuilt one out of old materials. But he has left an entire and elaborate structure as it was, and given it a new foundation. To drop metaphor, he had added to a contrapuntal movement on two subjects, a third subject which, from its surpassing dignity, situation, and treatment, seems not to have been added to them, but, as it were, to have taken them on to it. I cannot call to mind another instance of a similar proceeding. Every one will know the chorus " Wretched Lovers," and the wailing prophetic strain with which it opens.

Wretch - ed   lo - vers!

Those who know thus much will remember the stirring second subject on the words, " Behold the Monster Polyphème," and the counter subject, so different in character, on a fragment of the same phrase. In a set of thirteen " Chamber Duets" which Handel is said to have written during his stay in Hanover after his first visit to England, *i.e.*, in the year 1711, there is a movement which is made up of the second and third subjects of the chorus, but *without the first*. As an example of one of Handel's earlier productions, of which he evidently thought well, and which illustrates one of his modes of working, you will be interested perhaps in hearing it. The entire composition consists of three considerably developed movements, of which the following is the last.

DUET.—DAGL' AMORI FLAGELLATA.

From the "*Chamber Duets.*"   HANDEL.

rà, fug-gi-rà, fug-gi-rà, da gl'amo-re fia--gel-

rà, fug-gi-rà, fug-gi-rà, da gl'amo-re fia--gel-

la-ta la discordia fuggi-rà, fuggi-rà, fuggi-rà, da--gl'a-

la-ta la discordia fuggi-rà, fuggi-rà, fuggi-rà, da--gl'a-

--mo----ri fia----gel-la-ta, la discordia fuggi-

mo----ri fia------gel--la--ta,

rà, fuggirà, fuggirà,

la discordia fuggirà, fuggi - rà, fuggi-

da-gl'a - mo - ri fiagel - la - ta, fiagel - la - ta la dis-cordia fuggi -

rà, da-gl'a - mo - ri fiagel - la - ta, fiagel - la - ta la dis-cordia fuggi -

rà, fuggi - rà, fuggi - rà, la dis-cor - dia fug - gi-

rà, fuggi - rà, fuggi - rà, la dis-cor - dia fug - gi-

rà.

rà.

lampi e - terni spargerà, lampi e-terni spargerà.

. . . . lampi e-terni sparge-

lampi e - terni sparge - rà . . . .

rà, lampie e - terni sparge - rà . . . .

Bel - - la gio - ia in-a - mo - ra - tà, in - a - mo-

Bel - - - la gio - ia in-a - mo-

I have repeatedly called attention in this course to the fact that, though many very ingenious and interesting essays in instrumental music were made at very early epochs, the Second Period (the fifteenth and sixteenth centuries) owes, so to speak, all its interest for us—and even the Third Period with which we have been lately dealing, most of its interest—to its vocal compositions. Instrumental music has actually attained its present eminent or pre-eminent position—nay, I might say, it only began to attain it—within the memory of men living. Mendelssohn and Spohr were among us, as it seems, but the other day. These very meetings of ours have been honoured by the presence of a musician who knew and had received council from Beethoven. And I could name another who has actually seen, and even spoken with, Haydn. The epoch of Handel is, as you know, considerably anterior to this more recent and eminently instrumental or " symphonic" epoch. Handel was forty-seven years of age when Haydn was born ; and Mozart had only attained his third year when Handel's career was brought to a close. During the first half of the last century, a success in instrumental music at all equivalent to that of Handel in vocal music, was obviously not to be looked for. "Ample strides" are not altogether unfamiliar to the student of art history ; but the stride from Corelli to Beethoven was too ample even for the giant Handel. Moreover, it must always be remembered that the musical composer, unlike the poet or the painter, touches the public only through an intermediate agency ; and whatever Handel might have conceived, any musical conceptions demanding for their expression more than a very limited amount of executive skill must have waited many a long year before they could have been made intelligible to any public, and (I may add) before any public could have been found to whom they would have proved intelligible. Handel, to whom nothing in his art was alien or unfamiliar, wrote much instrumental music ; but it bears no comparison, either in quantity or quality, with his vocal music. Indeed no instrumental music of that epoch could possibly do so. But it would be a great mistake to suppose that, whatever it might be relatively, absolutely Handel's instrumental pieces are deficient in invention, science, or interest. On the contrary, some of them are among the comparatively few contemporary works of this kind that are still familiar even to the unlearned.

The "Pastoral Symphony" in "The Messiah," and the March in "Judas Maccabeus," would of course have kept their places in public estimation, in connexion with the two very popular oratorios of which they form part. But the Overture to the "Occasional Oratorio," and above all the "Dead March" in "Saul," are compositions which rest on their own individual merits; being known to comparatively few in their original positions, to almost everybody as single pieces.

I propose however, on the present occasion, to call your attention not to any pieces of this character, but to one or two of a class which Handel did much to raise to its present importance—music for keyed instruments.

The finger-board is a very ancient invention, and one of those inventions which, being of necessity governed by natural laws, attain perfection, in all essential points, at once. The average size of the human hand once ascertained, the average width of each key in the organ (to which keys were first applied) was necessarily determined with it. The keyed instruments of the years following the first invention of the finger-board, down to the latter part of the last century, differed from the pianoforte in the fact that the strings were acted upon, not by a hammer, but by a *plectrum*, which, by pulling the string out of its place, set it in vibration—as the strings of the harp or guitar are set in vibration by the finger. A still existing type of these instruments is presented in the mandolin, a little guitar still now and then heard in the streets. This class of instrument, the generic term for which is "clavichord" (*i.e.* stringed instrument with keys), attained perfection in the harpsichord, examples of which many of you perhaps have seen. For the harpsichord, on which Handel was a great performer, he wrote many pieces, which were published at intervals during his life, under the French title of "Pieces pour le Clavecin." The first Collection of these was published in 1720 ; the second in 1733. In the first is found the air with variations, since known as "The Harmonious Blacksmith." I say "since known" because the name does not appear in any edition of these Pièces published during Handel's life. Nor am I aware of any authority for the story which has been connected with it. There is nothing in itself improbable in the fact or fiction of a musician like Handel excogitating a tune out of the blows of a hammer, the chiming of bells, and the whistling of a blacksmith, either heard separately or all together. The tune has been attributed to a contemporary of Handel, Wagenseil, a very eminent performer on, and composer for, the harpsichord. But so many musical ideas—other people's, as well as his own—must always have been stored in Handel's memory, that he might very well be excused having forgotten, at times, who were their right owners. Be this as it may, the tune, though a very pretty one, owes all its celebrity to the variations that follow it, which variations are indisputably Handel's, and may be not unfitly compared to the tail of a comet, which, small as may be its specific gravity, fills the mind of the common observer with more wonder than does the body to which it owes its existence.

The so-called "Harmonious Blacksmith" is too familiar and too accessible to justify my introduction of it now. I prefer bringing before you another and a less familiar example of these Suites, or Series of movements. It is from No. 6 of the Second Book, the first movement of which is an "Allemande," the second a "Courante," the third and last a "Gigue"—all in G minor. You shall hear the "Courante."

COURANTE.

From "*Pièces pour le Clavecin*,"
2nd Col. No. 6.

HANDEL.

Courante.

We have had two specimens of Handel's earlier dramatic music. It will be interesting and instructive to compare with these one of much later date, from the opera "Sosarme," written and produced in 1732, *i.e.*, seven years before the termination of his copnexion with the Opera stage, and his entry on that new career which has made his name so widely known among, and so dear to, his countrymen by adoption. Here is an air, better known in connexion with some sacred words subsequently misfitted to it, than in its original form. Touching and graceful as is the melody, however allied, I greatly prefer it with the original words, which are words of consolation from a child to a mother. The notes are inspired by the very soul of tenderness and filial love.

This I shall follow by an example of Handel's songs of a very different class—a class of which as yet we have had no specimen, and to which I find it hard to give a distinctive name. It would have been strange had Handel left no record in his works of a certain humour, or rather playfulness of character, none the less real from having been kept in check by, or rather hidden under, a somewhat august if not austere manner. There is a song in the secular oratorio (if I may use such an expression) "Semele" (produced in 1743, the year subsequent to that in which the "Messiah" was first performed) which is sung by a somewhat unpromising vocalist, Somnus,— if not "in the intervals of business," at least in the intervals of his normal state; for it is a very lively song. Indeed it seems to me less characteristic of Somnus than of Handel himself at the time he wrote it; being just such a song as a gentleman of a certain age and portly presence might, under softening influences, throw off in an easy-going way. It is preceded by a short dialogue in recitative between Juno and Iris, which explains the situation and is in itself pleasing. It will, I think, be new to most of you.

AIR.—RENDI 'L SERENO.

From the Opera "*Sosarme.*"   HANDEL.

Rendi 'l se-reno al ci - - glio, Madre non pianger più, non pianger

più, no, Madre non pianger più. Ren -

- di 'l se - re - - no al ciglio, Madre non pianger più.

No,   no, Madre   non pianger più.

Te - mer d'al cun pe - ri - glio,

Og - gi come puoi tu og - - - gi, come puoi tu madre.

Dal Segno.

SCENE.

From Congreve's "*Semele.*"

Handel.

Recitative. (Soprano.)

(Iris.) Dull god! canst thou at-tend the wa-ter's fall, And not hear Sa-tur-nia's

call? (Juno.) Peace, I - ris! peace, I know how to charm him; Pa-si-

thea's name a-lone can warm him. Som-nus, a-rise! Dis-close thy ten-der

eyes; For Pa-si-the-a's sight Endure the light. Somnus, a-rise!

soft . . . . than a soft purl - ing stream, More sweet is that

name, More sweet is that name than a soft . . . . than a

· soft purl·ing· stream, More sweet . . . More sweet . . . is

that . . name, More sweet is that name than a soft purl - ing stream.

With pleasure, with plea-sure re - pose I'll for - sake, If

you'll grant me but her to soothe me a - wake . . . .

. . . . With pleasure, with pleasure re-

pose I'll for-sake, If you'll grant me but her to soothe me a - wake . .

. . . . to soothe me a - wake,

Da Capo.

If you'll grant me but her to soothe me a - wake.

Da Capo.

I have confined myself in this lecture almost exclusively to one view of Handel's genius and career, and this the least important, though perhaps not the least interesting, one. Of Handel the composer of "The Messiah" and "Israel in Egypt," it cannot be so necessary to say anything, to an English audience, as of Handel the industrious, versatile, and ready artist in operas, masques, ballets, concertos, sonatas, marches, gavots, hornpipes, fire-music, water-music, forest-music, and I know not what besides, and the thirty years' manager of a London Italian Opera House,—always (let this never be forgotten) the same honest, truth-telling, God-fearing man, who so becomingly gave his later years to compositions (as he himself said) better suited to the decline of life, and which he hoped would "not merely entertain his hearers but make them better."

Of Handel's influence on English musical composition I would willingly have spoken more fully ; but I have already trespassed too long on your indulgence. If I do so for a moment longer, it is that I may, in your presence, very heartily thank the Ladies and Gentlemen behind me—not forgetting those absent —for co-operation which has more than doubled any interest you may have taken in these lectures. What meets the public ear is the least part of the labour of those who address themselves to it ; and I feel that I have taxed the time and pains of my friends here very heavily. To you I may be permitted to express a hope that our present parting may not prove to have been final.

THE END.

CPSIA information can be obtained at www.ICGtesting.com
Printed in the USA
LVOW12s0915171013

357251LV00002B/117/P

9 781108 063982